My Heart Has
Seventeen Rooms

THE MACMILLAN COMPANY
NEW YORK • CHICAGO
DALLAS • ATLANTA • SAN FRANCISCO
LONDON • MANILA

IN CANADA
BRETT-MACMILLAN LTD.
GALT, ONTARIO

My Heart Has Seventeen Rooms

by CAROL BARTHOLOMEW

THE MACMILLAN COMPANY

New York 1959

First Printing

Library of Congress catalog card number: 59–7969

The Macmillan Company, New York
Brett-Macmillan Ltd., Galt, Ontario

Printed in the United States of America

For Gurbux Singh Babbar, F.R.C.S.
with
continuing affection and gratitude

ACKNOWLEDGMENTS

I would like to express my appreciation to the officers and men of the Government of the Punjab for their kindness and courtesy toward us during our stay in India.

I would also like to thank Mr. Harvey Slocum for giving us the opportunity to work at Bhakra; Mrs. Rudolph Erickson, my mother-in-law, for her interest and continual encouragement with this book; Dr. Alfred Fisk, and Miss Marie Merkle, who made much of this possible fourteen years ago; and my dear husband and children, despite whom I finally got it written.

AUTHOR'S NOTE

In the spring of 1954, my husband Bart signed a contract with the Government of the Punjab to work as an Engineer on Bhakra Dam, in Northern India. In June of the same year we traveled out to India with our three children, Stephen age 6, Tony age 4, and the baby, Nathan, who was a year old.

This book is a journal of the years we spent in India, and more especially a journal of the time I spent in the seventeen-room Indian hospital which became the heart of my life there. This book does not pretend to give a picture of life in India. It is only the story of a few years spent, in one tiny corner of a very large country, by an American family. Nor is this book meant to represent the views of other Americans who may have been there at the same time.

Now we are working on another dam, in a different country, but those seventeen rooms, and the people who occupied them, still remain a part of my heart.

CAROL BARTHOLOMEW

one

Our trip is over. We have arrived at the far north of the Indian Punjab, in the small town which houses all the Indian and American families brought here to build the most challenging dam in the world. Here the Indian government is pledged to jump over the centuries and construct the largest dam yet attempted, in an area almost untouched by our atomic age. I feel already that I could write pages and pages filled with nothing but impressions—no opinions—just color and noise and people. This land of temples and turbans certainly lives up to its reputation.

We caught a train in the old Delhi station for the last 250 miles. The station, a huge dim cavern peopled with Indians of every description, was like a crowded dream. Women nursed their babies, while more babies crawled about among mounds of luggage, and more women cooked supper, or washed clothes at the water taps. Men slept everywhere, while others ran shouting over ramps, piles of luggage on their heads.

The final lap of the journey was like no train ride we had ever taken. Our private compartment was barred and locked, windows and doors, inside and out. Dire warnings were given us to open no door under any circumstance until Nangal was reached. At every station along the way, people pounded and

cried out for us to open and let them enter. Looking through
the bars out into the dark night, we could see mobs of Indians
up and down the tracks; men, women and tiny children, trying
to force their way onto the already crowded train. Hands
reached through our windows, or clutched at the bars, while
men pleaded with us, in broken English, to let them ride. I
could imagine how exhausted the women must be, and the
children, and would certainly have crowded our compartment
full, if I had been alone. For the last fifty miles, we could hardly
see out of the windows because of the men clinging by fingers
and toes to the outside of the car. Every time the train rounded
a curve, Bart and I held our breath, while the men outside
clung even tighter and screamed to each other. The boys, of
course, were puzzled by our concern, and kept up a refrain of,
"But why can't we ride outside, too? But why not? We can
hold tight, daddy!"

But our trip is over. Friends from former jobs met us at the
station. They fed us breakfast, lunch and dinner, filled our
ears with news and views of India, and helped us settle in. Now
we are all enjoying our first quiet hours, and the chance to
look around us at what will be our home for several years to
come.

We are surrounded here by a fairly high range of hills with
rugged contours, dry, but covered with scrub and some trees.
The river valley where Nangal is situated is arid, semidesert.
Erosion has worn the land into a series of low mesas separated
by deep, rocky gullies. From the air it must look like a jig-saw
puzzle.

The river winds down through the flat lands from the mountains above, cutting the deep gorge where Bhakra Dam is being
built. Right now there is not much water in the river, but the
banks are so wide and sandy that I can see how it must spread
over the landscape during the rainy season.

Our houses are very comfortable. From the outside they look like brick barracks, or small forts. They are built with thick walls, square lines and flat tar roofs. Since much the same type of construction has been used throughout the town, and there is very little foliage, it gives the rather desolate impression of some sort of Army installation. We all have large yards with ample space for flower and vegetable gardens, since the houses are set well apart from each other. Each area of a block or two is enclosed by a wire fence with various gates. This is called a compound.

I was disappointed to find that all the Americans are housed together in three adjacent compounds. I was hoping we might have Indian neighbors. I should think our relations with each other might be better if our housing were not so segregated. However, other Americans tell me that this was tried, and it was an Indian decision to change. Maybe we weren't very good neighbors!

Our bungalow, when we arrived, was surrounded by hopeful job applicants. It was hard to disappoint any of them, but obviously there is a limit to the number of servants one family can use or afford. Our cook had already been hired for us by friends. His name is Ram, and he is special, having worked for another American family, who trained him in our ways of cooking. Also he speaks good English, which is helpful.

Most of the Americans here have picked up enough Hindi and Punjabi to make themselves fairly well understood. I have borrowed a Hindi book, the only one available, which concerns itself only with names of things, and direct orders: "Pick up my shoes," "Make the bed," and so forth. This is not precisely the thing for social intercourse, but perhaps I will be able to remedy that later.

I also hired a gardener, who for about eight dollars a month does all the gardening, keeps up the lawn and grows our vegetables. The cook is paid about twenty-one dollars a month, plus the right to occupy one of our two servants' quarters. He does all the cooking, serving, grocery shopping and dishes. We also have a sweeper who does most of the heavier cleaning and scrubbing, and a dhobi who takes care of the washing and ironing. The only other servant I will need (?) is someone to help with the children, but I want to wait until I can find one really capable.

All the servants "mem-sahib" me like mad, with a little bow and their hands to their foreheads. This makes me feel I should bow back, or at least say, "Thank you," but I suppose I will get used to it.

What I will be doing while everyone else works still remains to be seen. But I have been waiting for an opportunity like this for a long time, and I do not want to waste a moment of it. I hope that our family, by our collective actions and attitudes, can let the Indians know that we like them and like their country. For my part, I want to do some kind of medical social work during my hours of free time, since that kind of work interests me and I have had some small training in the field. I want to work in the hospital here if I can prove that I really wish to be useful, and if they will accept me.

There seems to be a good deal of tension between the Indians and Americans, and also among the Americans themselves. The Americans have been extremely nice to us, especially those we had known before. But I think I detect in their solicitude a silent, but mutual compassion for another little lamb being led to the slaughter. My enthusiasm for things Indian is met by an exchange of glances, and a "Well, you will find out." I understand that a group of Americans was sent home rather abruptly a short while ago, and this seems to be the main cause of the ill feeling toward the Indians. I want to form my own opinions, so I will continue to be enthusiastic, and make my own mistakes.

The friction between the various Americans here does not surprise me. Like most construction camps, this one is a small town in miniature, and subject to the usual rumors, gossip and conflict that exist whenever too few people are too much together. I expect I have already said or done something which will be under discussion by tomorrow.

There are about thirty-five American advisers here. Several are bachelors, but all the married personnel have their families with them, including children of various ages. About a quarter of this group are old neighbors, with whom we worked on Bull Shoals Dam in Arkansas. These friends and many others here are mostly natives of Arkansas. The majority of the rest are from California. We are in a middle position, having worked in Arkansas but hailing from the West Coast. As a group, we represent a very typical cross section of skilled American labor. There are only a few college degrees among us, and our husbands' qualifications rest in years of experience and a lot of hard work. Apparently the job of the Americans is to try to fill the gap which exists between Indian engineers and completely unskilled coolies. We are to teach our essential crafts of heavy construction: drilling, blasting, tunneling, iron work, steel erection and all the rest, to as many Indian workmen as possible. At the same time the dam is already in the process of being built. So the Americans responsible for each branch of the work must push and prod and continually supervise to keep the schedule. It is a heavy load for so few men, and filled with frustrations and discouragements, from what we are told.

The town here is fascinating, and not, as I feared, depressing. This is a model town built by the Indians to serve the needs of all those working on the dam. There are a hospital and several schools. When the dam was first begun, the laborers were all living in the typical north Indian mud huts, but now most of them live in more adequate dwellings. These look like long lines of small brick motels. Each has one or two rooms, and an enclosed patio-type rear yard. Most of the quarters have electricity and some even have plumbing although the latrines and water taps scattered through the town serve most of the people. For India, all of this is most advanced, although by our standards it is marginal indeed.

I had to go to the bazaar almost at once to buy the linens, dishes and so forth necessary to setting up the house. We have two Indian-style bazaars or shopping centers where we will do all our buying. Both are several blocks long and consist of tiny shops, one after another, dealing in every conceivable type of merchandise. I wandered from one to the other, buying an item here and an item there. Some shops are dusty little cubbyholes filled with sacks of dried beans and peas with strings of herbs dangling from the ceiling. In others, semi-naked men sit in the midst of the most gorgeous profusion of silks and satins. There are more modern booths, their shelves lined with boxes of soap flakes and tins of cigarettes, and shops with elaborate displays of highly decorated, sticky Indian sweets—the effect somewhat spoiled by the clouds of flies and yellow jackets hovering above them. There are tea stalls from which the aroma of curry and chilis, as I passed, was nearly overpowering. Many of the booths are filled with rather limp vegetables, where the wandering cows make every attempt to nudge the turnips from my hand. The most fun of all are the little grab-bag stalls which display everything from broken teakettles to gaudy religious calendars. Here I could find almost anything: bent nails and glass bracelets, old books and bright balloons, firecrackers and wool socks, all jumbled together in magnificent confusion.

Our buying trip today was rather in the nature of a royal procession, since we were followed from booth to booth by a horde of children and many grown men. I am told this is not unusual, but more pronounced today since everyone knows we are newcomers. Being the object of so many curious stares and whispered comments is very disconcerting. But the Indian children behaved so much as ours might under similar circumstances that I felt it was very funny. First there would be whispers and giggling, soon joined by nudges and pushing. Then one little boy would be in the forefront with his hand to his head and an impertinent look on his face. He would say, "Guda morning, Mem-sahib. OK!" and then run off, followed by shouts of laughter from the others. This little drama was repeated over and over, a never-ending source of amusement to the crowd.

two

To someone accustomed to the clatter of traffic, the sounds here on a summer night are strangely new. The air is still and heavy. Above my head a ceiling fan is revolving slowly, sending hot gusts through the room. It has a nice soothing hum, until it gets off balance, when it clanks and stutters like an old model T. Then I wonder if these things ever fall, and try to figure out which portion of my anatomy it will be most likely to hit.

Close by the house, the servants are gathered around their beds, talking quietly and sharing a good-night smoke. In the lower yard the frogs are providing a basso profundo chorus for a few highly original solo efforts. These are not the nice, little country-gentlemen frogs that we have at home, but great green monstrosities who look like the pictures in fairy tales of enchanted princes.

A loud-speaker in the bazaar is blaring out Indian music. If it were nearby, I know the voice would sound nasal and strident, but filtered through the air, I hear only the melody, with that oriental quality westerners find so haunting. Across the river I hear the perpetual *tink-tink* of a gristmill as it turns round and round grinding someone's wheat. It sounds like a tiny bell being rung at measured intervals.

A man is walking down the road playing a tune on a reed

pipe. The faint, high notes of the reed are more soothing than those which the cook across the way is making as he tries to teach himself to play the bagpipes.

Soon we will be treated to our nightly rodeo, since I hear the heavy breathing and crunching of jaws which signal us that the cows are in the garden again. During the daytime these marauders are removed from the yard with quiet dispatch by a few pebbles. But at night the sound of a cow seems to fill the servants with virtuous rage, and is the signal for a great chase in which everyone, men and cows, run about the yard full tilt, shattering the air with murderous yells and tormented mooing. The servants from the neighbors' houses join in with shouted advice, while the poor confused animals lumber blindly onto the veranda, into the fence, and finally out of the gate. I suppose having the cows get in at night represents the chance for a lark—something to relieve the monotony—certainly the servants appear to enjoy the whole thing thoroughly. But, if they are trying to impress us with their courage and devotion to duty by all this, the effect is completely spoiled by our knowledge that they left the gate wide open in the first place. Maybe closing the gate to keep the cows out is just the sort of uninteresting solution that would occur only to an American.

My relationship with the servants has not yet progressed beyond the point of guarded mutual appraisal. They work with tremendous industry, one eye on me searching for a reaction. For my part, I exert myself to be courteous, appreciative, and the ideal "mem-sahib." I have received a good deal of well meant but highly conflicting advice from some of the other Americans, old hands at this mem-sahib business, on how to handle the servant problem. Personally, to find myself the proud possessor of a "servant problem" strikes me as so hilarious that I am afraid my attitude lacks the gravity considered proper to the situation.

I have run into my first snag with the gardener, or "mali" as he is called. He is the most engaging boy, with a great big grin

which splits his face in two. I had noticed that he was darker
and wore different clothes from the rest, in this case an elab-
orately draped loincloth—nothing else. Now I discover that he
is from a different part of India and completely ignorant of the
languages spoken here. That means none of us can talk to him,
nor can he make himself understood, even to the other servants.
This will certainly have the result of giving him a free hand with
the garden. So far his work has consisted of diligently applying
whitewash to every rock and stone in our part of the compound,
and arranging them in neat little circles around each growing
plant—mostly weeds—and, of course, chasing cows. But he
performs these functions with such enthusiasm and beaming
good humor that even if I knew the words to fire him, I
wouldn't have the heart.

Ram, the cook, has a very sweet disposition, and a very
grumpy expression. He answers everything I say with, "han."
This is a Hindi word meaning, "yes," but from the inflection
he gives it, I hear "maybe" and even "That's what you think!"
on occasion. When he does not agree with me, he goes into the
kitchen and mutters furiously under his breath. Ram is extremely independent, while the sweeper, Jugetram, is meek,
mild and humble in a groveling sort of way. Even though I
understand the reasons why former untouchables behave this
way, I find myself reacting with impatience, thinking, "Why
don't you stand up and act like a man!"

I made my first visit to the hospital today and came away
with some confused impressions. The hospital compound is
right next to ours, separated from our house only by a narrow
road and two fences. The hospital is built in the shape of the
letter E. The two legs of the letter form the male ward and the
female and children's wards respectively. The back of the E
contains the doctors' offices, outpatients' clinic and the X-ray
rooms. The small center leg holds the operating theater and
anesthesia rooms. The building is constructed of stained, un-

painted concrete over mud, is one story tall, and is surrounded on all sides by wide verandas.

The hospital yard, as I walked through, was filled with hordes of people engaged in every kind of activity. There were mothers nursing babies, and more babies crawling about underfoot, their fat bare bottoms elevated. Some of the men crouched on their haunches eating, while a few feet away another, with his back turned, was urinating into the shrubbery. Others simply lay on the ground, eyes shut, as though already dead. There were even several goats and a cow wandering about nibbling the grass.

Inside, every room was filled with beds, and there were many more lining each veranda. Some of the patients were strolling aimlessly about, while those confined to bed were surrounded by dozens of anxious relatives. There were several little men on their hands and knees, mopping at the floor with filthy-looking wet rags, and others energetically polishing the brass door handles. The doctors' offices were crowded to suffocation with patients, all apparently talking at once. It was terribly hot, and the whole place was filled with a miasma compounded of perspiration, urine, disinfectant, and that awful odor of sick flesh. The entire thing is so unlike any hospital I have ever been in, that it is difficult to be objective.

They must certainly need another pair of free hands, if the crowded conditions I saw today are typical. I cannot think of a better way of getting to know the people here, how they live and what they are like. I want to work there more than ever.

Our boys have jumped into life here without a backward glance. The fact that they are friendly and so gregarious has presented a problem I hardly know how to handle. The hospital compound and the labor quarters behind it are swarming with children. As soon as my kids leave the house, these small Indians come over, under, and through the fence, descending on us like locusts. Many are bright, engaging and sweet, but all are extremely dirty and quite possibly contagious. Our servants have all had physical examinations, but I can hardly demand a health certificate from every Indian the children come in contact with. Nor can I make any move to chase the children away. We have spent long hours with the boys discussing how to behave in someone else's country, and the importance of being friendly and polite to everyone. So, if I am less than friendly myself at any time, they will certainly be aware of it. A prejudiced adult may conceal his true feelings with tact and discretion when dealing with others, but prejudiced children are cruel and rude indiscriminately. I will not have my children thinking of Indians as "dirty ragheads," no matter what the alternative. However, the alternative is not pleasant to contemplate when Tony strolls by arm in arm with a particularly tubercular-looking boy, or when, as happened yesterday, the baby runs out the front door, and straight into the arms of a pathetically foul beggar.

None of the household appliances which we shipped from the States, before leaving, will arrive for some time. So we are living here without many of the things Americans consider necessities. We do have a small refrigerator rented to us by the government. The dhobi washes our clothes in the river, pounding them on stones in the Indian fashion. Ram is cooking all our meals over a small charcoal fire. This looks fairly easy, but it is Ram's secret how he gets the fire to burn. My attempts to heat a pot of coffee resulted in stinging smoke, but no flame. Each of the American houses has a hot water heater, something extremely rare even among wealthy Indians. So I cannot claim that we are existing under primitive conditions by any means. Actually the lack of some of the modern conveniences does not bother me a bit—someone else is doing all the work!

The food here is quite adequate, if one keeps an open mind. Our meat is mainly goat, which we hopefully call "mutton." There is also pork, but there was a scandal several months back when all the stray dogs in town disappeared just as the slaughterhouse declared a pork surplus! Since few of us are able to be quite *that* hopeful, we don't eat much pork.

This is the hottest time of the year, just before the monsoons start, and also the worst season for finding fresh fruit and vegetables in the bazaar. We do have onions, tomatoes, okra, carrots and cucumbers, and several delicious fruits. The bananas are only about three inches long and look green, since they are tree ripened. There are many different varieties of mangoes, but these have such a distinctive flavor that none of us, except Nate the baby, has come to like them yet. Nate devours them with the same "oh" of satisfaction he gives ice cream. The apples are only about an inch in diameter but make good pies. Besides cake, pies and cookies, Ram also bakes all our bread and rolls. These have a distinctive coarse texture, since Indian flour is heavy and rough. I enjoy most of the food, and it is heaven not to have to plan the meals or cook them myself.

three

For two weeks now the sun has been blazing even more vividly in the sky. The ground is cracked and parched; all the trees and plants are dusty and limp. In the villages the buffalo water holes have been reduced to sticky green slime. Even the people look shriveled and dry. The heat has been so intense it seems to draw every particle of moisture from every living thing, until, wherever I look, I see only burned earth and panting animals moving in shimmering waves of heat.

Last night the monsoon came. How dull mere rain will seem after this! First there is a stillness in the air that seems to go on and on. Everything is motionless and silent, as though the whole world had stopped breathing. Then the wind starts pushing and churning the air about with immense force. It blows through the house, slamming doors and windows, knocking over vases, and shoving all the heat from its path. Then the lightning begins, each flash outlining in silver the storm clouds piled above us. Then the noise of the thunder pounding, the crows screaming, the buffalo moaning, the voices of many people, is blown to us by the wind. Running like ants in all directions, trying to find shelter before the rain, men and women call to each other in great good humor. Now comes the rain: the wettest rain you ever saw, solid walls of water which conceal the surrounding landscape and smash against the earth. In a few seconds the dry cracked ground is inches deep in mud, and soon the whole land is one large lake. When the storm is over, everything seems clean and fresh. The air has a new smell, a new taste; even the stars look scrubbed.

I am going to the hospital every day, although I have not done much more than learn my way around and identify a few of the patients and staff by sight. The head of the hospital, Dr. Babbar, has been very nice, but formal. I have the impression that he does not have a high opinion of "do-gooders." There is a great deal I do not understand, and about a million questions I would like answered. I feel critical about many things, but I try to remember that I am also very ignorant of conditions here. Sometimes I feel that some of the staff members are trying to test my reactions. They lead me to the dirtiest, most miserable patients, then watch me for any sign of distaste. But perhaps I am mistaken, and they are only showing off what they consider the "sights" of the hospital.

This morning they brought a girl to me. I had noticed her before because she always has a bandage around her jaw and head, like the ones used in the funnies to indicate a toothache. One of the nurses spoke to her, and she pulled away the bandage and showed her face to me. Her whole cheek and part of her jaw were gone leaving an open hole through which I could see her inner mouth and tongue. It is hard not to reveal the shock you feel when confronted by something totally unexpected and pitiable, and I am not sure I always succeed. But no one could bear to hurt, in any way, people already so miserable. Any initial feeling of repugnance is replaced at once by honest concern.

I have learned a little more about the purpose and organization of the hospital. It is a district hospital, maintained primarily to serve all the men working at Bhakra and their families, and particularly to care for any accident cases from the dam. Most of the available services are free to the patients. Since there is no other good hospital for nearly a hundred miles in any direction, it must also care for people from the many surrounding villages who need help. Already I have decided that this is a good hospital. Despite conditions here and a complete lack of many of the things considered necessities in our hospitals, I am told that this one is really outstanding by Indian standards. Originally it was built to hold about seventy beds, but as people have become increasingly aware of its existence, more and more villagers are carried in for treatment, until there are beds lining every available corridor and veranda. Besides these serious cases that require hospital care, the outpatient clinic treats from three hundred to five hundred people a day.

In charge of the entire hospital is Dr. Gurbux Babbar, who is called the Chief Medical Officer. His work consists of inspecting and directing the hospital and several outlying clinics, supervising the staff, the treatment of all cases, performing all surgery, examining all accident and serious cases personally, handling all the paperwork needed to maintain the facilities, and acting as personal physician to all the American advisers, Indian engineers and their families. Under him, at the hospital, are six other doctors, two women and four men. One woman and one man care for the inpatients, and another couple care for the outpatients. One doctor is an X-ray and anesthesia specialist, and the last handles the laboratory facilities. Working under the doctors are seven nurses and five men called dispensers (who seem to be like the Navy pharmacist mates), a number of men called ward servants, who act as nurses' aids, and many sweepers who are in charge of cleanliness and all bedpan care. At first sight the staff of workers seems large, but it is actually very inadequate and poorly trained to care for the high percentage of critical cases admitted here.

The hospital is full of diseases hardly ever seen in the United States. Typhoid, diphtheria, tetanus, malaria are all killers here. Tuberculosis and venereal disease are very widespread, and of course we see all the other ailments common to man all over the world. The degree of malnutrition among all the people makes any disease harder to withstand and more difficult to cure. An example of this problem is one man I am particularly concerned about.

He is a patient who was carried in from one of the villages just recently. I did not notice him for several days because his bed is at the end of the outside veranda, separated from the rest, and shrouded in fly-netting. But yesterday I walked down there, and what I saw made pictures of concentration camp victims very real to me. Lying on the bed was a naked collection of skin-covered bones surmounted by a skull, with lips pulled back in a perpetual grimace, and deeply sunken eyes. One leg was covered with stained bandages, and the stench coming from it was over-powering. I was so aghast that I risked making a nuisance of myself by asking to take his chart to Dr. Babbar and learn his story.

It seems that some time ago this man fell and suffered multiple compound fractures of his lower leg. These were never properly set, the circulation in his leg was impaired, and infection started. He was not brought to the hospital until it appeared likely he was dying, and by this time his whole leg, including the bone, was rotten and septic. He is also suffering from hookworm, chronic malaria, anemia and malnutrition. Dr. Babbar says he has almost reached the point of no return. The only thing that might save him is an immediate amputation, but his hemoglobin is only 20 per cent, and there is no one either able or willing to donate blood. I think I know someone who may be both, but it might take a little fast talking.

Away from the hospital the days go by filled with entertaining incidents. So many things delight me here, for instance, all the animals that live in the house. We have dozens of tiny lizards, toads, and even field mice, nearly tame. In the evening when the lights attract the bugs, the lizards skitter here and there over the walls and ceiling, while the toads hop about, blinking at us and looking very wise. Nate considers them his personal playthings and spends happy minutes wobbling about trying to catch one.

Out of the window I can watch a man pedal by on a bicycle, balancing a whole bed on his head, or see a tall, bearded Sikh pass, cradling in his arms a tired buffalo calf. Or a sadhu, daubed with saffron and ashes, will stand in front of my door preaching a sermon in Urdu to me, and sounding precisely like a southern evangelist. A constant procession of peddlers comes and goes all day, selling ice, fruit, peanuts, buffalo milk, chickens and even balloons. They each have a different cry by which they identify their wares—like our old "rags-and-bottles" man in the States.

The physical variety of the people here surpasses anything I ever expected. One has a tendency to think of eastern peoples as all looking alike, but it is not so. In Nangal, we have many handsome Sikhs. With their turbans off, and their hair falling around their shoulders, they look like a collection of Biblical prophets. Some of the Kashmiri people are ruddy, like dark Scots, with freckles and a reddish tinge to their hair. We also see Tibetans and Nepalese who are stockier and have Mongolian eyes. Skin color varies from white to a deep mahogany brown. Even hair and eye color varies. A grass cutter who works nearby has a tousle-headed little daughter who is blonde and blue-eyed. The facial structure of the Hindus is narrower through the forehead and wider around the jaw than ours. This is apt to give them a heavy, petulant expression when their faces are in repose. But most of them have delicately molded features, eyes full of fire, and sensitive, mobile lips. In fact, beside the Indians, we look like cornstarch pudding.

The other day was Lord Krishna's birthday, similar to our Christmas. The town was filled with holy men, sadhus and gurus, in every conceivable degree of nakedness. Best of all an immense elephant arrived to join the celebration. Several American fathers got together and hired the animal for two hours to give rides to all the American kids. It was really a tremendous beast, the biggest I have ever seen, and easily carried half a dozen children, with a couple of adults to hang onto them. One group of kids would pile on, clinging for dear life, while the elephant plodded around the compound, chased by the rest of the youngsters loudly demanding their turn. Everyone was excited except the elephant.

In India, the phrase "mind your own business" seems to have absolutely no meaning. Everyone minds everyone else's business. Privacy is apparently unvalued. Hence if anything in the least out of the way happens, you can count on attracting a milling mob of people who come to see what is going on. So it was with the elephant. First there were just the Americans and some of the servants' families, but before long half of Nangal was in the compound, gleefully watching the spectacle of "those crazy Americans riding around on an elephant." Our kids loved the ride, but couldn't see why we didn't just keep him around permanently, since two hours was not nearly time enough.

The children and I got our first look at Bhakra the other night. Bart drove us out just at dusk. The road from Nangal to the dam site, some seven miles long, is a narrow two-lane affair which winds up and around through the mountain range, then careens down the other side, in a series of terrifying curves. As you come around the last bend, the whole construction site is suddenly spread before you. Much of the equipment is brilliantly lighted, and strung between the two sides of the deep river gorge is a rope of lights—high up where the finished dam will one day be. I doubt that the dam will ever be as lovely as this flickering illusion.

Bhakra is being built in the steep, narrow ravine cut by the river Sutlej. The contours of the two mountainsides have been formed by the passage of the river, but the eroding action of the terrific monsoons has also done its bit. The bluffs are very steep, and where the channel has worn through it has left bare rocky cliffs with no vegetation. The rain pounding against these cliffs has washed out the softer rock, leaving the faces of the two mountains serrated into many knifelike ledges and sharp ridges. They look like two saw blades end on end facing each other. There is practically no flat area around the dam site, so more ledges have been blasted out of the mountains for offices, equipment and shops, with abruptly twisting roads built to reach them. At night, only partially illuminated and filled with grotesque machines, the whole landscape has a fantastic dreamlike quality. All of the equipment and buildings seem to teeter precariously on the very edge of space.

From the standpoint of foundations few dams have ever been attempted in such difficult terrain. The earth under the river bed and the surrounding mountains are all crisscrossed with seams and cracks deep in their interior. The grouting plant works night and day pumping cement deep into the endless crevasses. We drove up the right abutment to see this plant, circling round and round through silent arroyos and empty rock shelves. At the top of the mountain, on the very cliff's edge, we came abruptly on several large scaffoldings which seemed to be crowded with nothing but hundreds of dark eyes. Because they were so precisely the color of their surroundings, it took us several seconds to realize that the eyes belonged to men. Then we could see that the unbroken dusty grayness was made up of many figures, moving and working, all of them thickly powdered from head to foot with cement dust.

I am getting impatient with people who begin a sentence, "These Indians are so lazy—or dishonest—or stupid," then proceed to relate a few harassing incidents. They remind me of our Tony, who loudly proclaims that he has been bitten by a *million* mosquitoes, then proudly displays one itchy spot. One woman here told me, "Carol, you will like the Indians. Individually they are wonderful, but collectively they are hopeless." This has a nice catchy sound with a ring of conviction, but it doesn't really mean anything. There is simply no such thing as people collectively, and certainly not three hundred and ninety million people. Humans are not stones which will permit themselves to be collected into one big rock pile and judged as a single object. If only I can continue to keep in mind that India is a particular geographic area, inhabited by a group of individual human beings, all as different as we ourselves! If the Indians could think the same way when dealing with the group of people they clump together as "Americans," they might find that we are really not so bad either.

I am watching our baby, Nate, through the window as he takes his morning walk. He toddles all over the compound and is escorted, at the moment, by our cook, the cook next door, two gardeners and the sweeper. All the servants here adore him and are delighted when they have a chance to play with him. The fact that he goes to each of them so affectionately pleases them. And Ram behaves like a doting grandma, bragging about "his" baba outrageously and spoiling him to death with cookies and attention. What a shame that our State Department cannot recruit several thousand babies to fill their diplomatic posts! What a wonderful job they do of loving everyone, with the added bonus of being unable to make silly speeches!

four

Bart says I am being very generous with *his* blood, but he has agreed to give my man with the bad leg a transfusion. Dr. Babbar says that three or four transfusions would be better, and keeps warning me that it may well be too late to save him, no matter what we do. But he will surely die within a few days unless the amputation is attempted, so we will take Bart's red blood tomorrow, and Dr. Babbar will operate.

I am becoming more and more interested in many of the patients. The hospital staff leaves me pretty much alone to do as I please. What I do is not very much. Every morning I spend a few minutes visiting with each patient. Many speak at least some English, and I have learned to say in Punjabi the phrase, "How are you feeling?" also several words for different parts of the body, and the vital sentence, "I will speak to the doctor about you." My accent is atrocious, and is capable of sending a whole ward into raucous laughter. Once or twice I have misled a patient into thinking I really knew the language, and been engulfed with his rapid conversation, much to my dismay. The only purpose of these daily chats is to make the patients feel that someone is interested in them. They all believe that because I am an American I am a very important person with unlimited influence. Therefore, if I am concerned about their progress, they think I will use this influence to ensure their recovery. They are being given every care that is possible or available under these conditions, but if my interest and attention reassure them the visits can do no harm.

None of the doctors or nurses here has much "bedside manner." This is partly because they are so rushed and overworked, partly because most of the patients come from the "ignorant" masses, and are on a totally different social level from most of the staff. So although I am certain the doctors view each patient as a human being to be helped if possible, they have little respect for his intelligence or standards. The educated Indian's conviction that illiteracy presupposes stupidity is one of his worst faults. This attitude leads the doctors to make abrupt examinations, ask some brusque questions, discuss the case in English over the patient's prostrate form, and walk off. Frequently they leave the patient totally in the dark concerning what is wrong with him and what treatment is to be given. The staff members tell me that most of the cases are too ignorant to understand an explanation anyway. Indeed, most of the people appear used to such coldness, but it continually bothers me.

The fertility of this country is amazing. Before the monsoon started, everything was dry, brown and dusty. The few flowers looked as though they had been dried and pressed. Our house had no growing things around it except withered tufts of grass. We planted frail little vines, and almost overnight, since the rains started, they are trailing their creepers clear up on the roof and, clinging to the brick, have traveled around the house in every direction and ornamented it with a pale purple flower like a morning glory. Every place where we planted a single seed there is now a riot of color. After each rain the plants shoot up inches and blossom in an orgy of profusion. The flowers here are all helter-skelter. Some seem to suit India, matching the vitality and vividness of the people and countryside—great yellow sunflowers, brilliant orange daisies, and bushes covered with tiny cerise buds. Other plants look as though they should by rights be blooming in some English spinster's garden. We have a shrub called "touch-me-not" which is the most delicate plant I have ever seen, with pale apple-green leaves and, hidden beneath in clusters, tiny pastel petals. This shrub simply doesn't belong here.

After the first rain, the gardener ceased whitewashing rocks to build an elaborate waterway of dikes and ditches throughout the garden. This he tends ardently, flooding first one then another portion of the yard. There are shoots coming up too, though what they are I have no idea.

The baby gives our poor gardener endless trouble. Nate has become an awful little tease, and loves to head for the garden, full speed, and jerk up a tender new plant, one eye on the mali the whole time to see what he will do. The mali always comes through with an anguished, "Ney, baba." If the poor man starts for the scene of the crime, this is all the incentive Nate needs to start galloping through the rows of vegetables, laughing like mad and leaving havoc in his wake. When the mali finally catches him, they sit down on the grass together, and the mali gives "baba" a long lecture in Gujarati. Nate makes such earnest sounds in reply that I am sure the mali thinks he is talking back in English. It is quite a sight: the mali, black as the dirt he digs, wrapped in his elaborate loincloth, and Nate, blond and grinning, carrying on this two-way conversation with mutual head shaking and gestures.

The traditional Indian greeting here is made by putting the palms of the hands together, as if praying, bowing the head very slightly, and saying a word which sounds like "Numusti." But many of the people, and most of the children, still use the old Muslim greeting of "Salaam," said with the back of the right hand at the forehead. The two-year-old daughter of the sweeper next door performs this salaam with such enthusiasm that she nearly knocks herself over. I try to return in kind any greeting given me. But occasionally I forget myself and simply wave. In India the American gesture of waving goodbye means "Come here." This leads to confusion on both sides. I gaily wave to a group of children, and they dash toward me expectantly, then I realize my mistake and wonder what to do next. The children politely wait for me to tell them what I want, while I frantically go through my limited vocabulary, trying to remember a few words and unable to think of anything at all appropriate. Usually the impasse is broken by handing them some coins and pointing toward the sweet shop.

Ram, our cook, is waging a silent one-man campaign against me. He wants me to promote our present sweeper, Jugetram, to the position of "bearer," and give him charge of the children. This would entail a raise in pay for Jugetram, and permission to move his family into our remaining servants' quarter. Also it means I would have to hire another sweeper. This has been arranged by Ram also—it seems that Jugetram's wife's brother needs work. Ram's intrigues to bring all this about are very funny. He will come into the room where I am typing, leading Jugetram by the hand, and proceed as follows: "Mem-sahib, you work too hard. Small baby much trouble, very naughty. Jugetram likes baba." With this Jugetram usually receives a good poke in the ribs and, blushing crimson, is heard to mumble, "O.K., Mem-sahib!" I remain unimpressed and say, "But Jugetram doesn't know how to take care of the baby, and besides he can't speak English." Ram shrugs in the grand manner, and blandly states, "I teach him." I promise to think about it, and return to business. But the next time I enter the kitchen a strange boy is there, energetically scrubbing the brass.

"Who is that, Ram?"

"Mem-sahib, this is brother to Jugetram's wife. He is very good sweeper. He is much sad you work so hard. He give help."

When I point out that we already have a sweeper, and inquire if I am paying a second one also, Ram assures me that only the boy's tender solicitude for my welfare has prompted him to help out. Later I glance from the window, and see a girl with two small children sitting in the middle of my lawn.

"Ram, who is that in the yard?"

"Mem-sahib, that is Jugetram's wife and his small boy and girl. They come to see you because you are very good lady. They like you much."

This is hard to believe since they have never seen me before, but I go out, say hello, and play with the children. Persinni, the wife, is thrown into such confusion that she pulls a scarf over her face and giggles with embarrassment. The girl is an adorable little pixy with mischief in her eyes, and Ram knows very well that, as the mother of three boys, I cannot resist little girls. I know that Ram will eventually get his own way. I was beaten the minute he began his campaign, but I am going to hold out a day or two longer just to see what he does next.

The bazaar merchants have certainly picked up American ideas of economics rapidly. The small Indian merchant usually charges, for his products, a different price to every purchaser— based on a lightning calculation of what the traffic will bear. Each purchase is accompanied by frenzied haggling on both sides. The shopowner mournfully insists that bankruptcy is only minutes away if he permits such prices, while the buyer insists that *he* is already bankrupt and cannot afford a cent more, even to feed his starving children. This continues until both are nearly in tears, but quite, quite satisfied. Much to the disgust and bewilderment of the bazaar shopkeepers, Americans simply don't understand the rules of this game at all. At times they pay the first price asked, then yell to the skies that they have been cheated. Or they may indicate a willingness to bargain only to get angry when the price drops three hundred per cent, and refuse to buy from such a "robber." Most confusing of all, these very rich Americans never have any cash. But there is a magic sentence, the repetition of which will persuade any American to purchase any amount of goods at any price. This sentence is, "Pay me next month!" We are all in debt to our eyelashes, and there are a dozen or so shrewd merchants in the bazaar who have caught on to American buying habits. These happy men smile when they see us coming, and sing out, "Mem-sahib, you can pay me anytime!"

The question of the relative honesty or dishonesty of the Indian shopkeeper is a knotty one. Many Americans are bitterly convinced that we are being cheated on every side, and use as proof the tremendous amount it costs us to live as compared to the Indians. There is no question that we are charged more for almost everything than the Indians have to pay. However, I do not believe that the markup, for us, is much more than the markup in the United States. The difference is that Indian merchants operate on a very small margin of profit when dealing with other Indians, but expect a large one when selling to us. And they are not very tactful in permitting us to realize this fact. Here we are aware of the amount of markup; at home we were not. Here we buy at the same old prices day after day; there we could indulge in special sales and come away with the glowing conviction that we were saving money. Merchants here have learned little of our advertising methods—thank goodness—hence there is no façade of "Store-Wide Bargains" or "Gigantic Sales." However, neither have they discovered those companions of credit buying, interest and carrying charges. I think we all save enough through paying no interest of any sort in our many charge accounts here to more than make up for any "cheating."

The first week I went to the hospital I discovered that they have only enough food to give out forty-five meals a day. All the remaining patients must have their food brought to them by relatives. Many get nearly nothing. I found a young boy with a fractured pelvis who appeared to be receiving very little food, and decided to bring him two meals a day from our home. There does not seem to be anything wrong with this on the surface, but it has proved to be very poor judgment on my part. The first day, when I brought over a dinner of meat and vegetables, the boy's old father crawled across the floor to kiss my feet. This was a terribly embarrassing ordeal. My mistake was in picking a boy in a ten-bed ward. When I bring in the food, nine other pairs of eyes watch me and watch the food, focusing on every mouthful. The man in the next bed finally turned his face away and closed his eyes. I questioned the nurse, and sure enough, this man was receiving one glass of milk a day from the Red Cross, nothing else except the scraps other patients gave him. So I brought enough for both of them, but I am still very much aware of the remaining eight. I can't possibly feed them all. I will continue with these two until they leave, but I won't start it again. Better to bring several dozen hard boiled eggs, and give one to each.

five

We took Bart's blood for the transfusion and rationed it to our man drop by drop, one third before the operation, one third during, one third after. Even so, he was so weak we had trouble giving him the transfusion without throwing him into shock. Dr. Babbar gave me permission to watch the amputation, and explained to me, before he started, just what he would be doing. In this case, his objectives had to be speed and as little blood loss as possible, rather than a surgically perfect stump. The anesthetist refused to administer any kind of anesthesia unless Dr. Babbar would take full responsibility. This he did, cautioning me again about the small degree of hope existing and warning me not to count on success.

I was so frightened by the time the operation started that my legs would hardly hold me up. I have watched operations before, but never an amputation. However, once in the operating theater, I was so worried about the patient that I forgot to notice much of what was going on. Even with the transfusion, he was in an alarming condition. His pulse jumped about, weak and irregular, his blood pressure dropped down and down, and his breathing stopped for seconds at a time. Dr. Babbar continued working with deliberate haste, but gave out running instructions to the rest of us at the same time: "He is turning blue; push on his chest; make him breathe. Don't let his heart stop. Give him Coramine. Start some glucose in his other arm. Speed up the blood." It was all over very quickly, but I was exhausted with tension.

Our man survived the operation, but we still have to worry about the postoperative shock, and then, whether or not the stump will heal properly. He has taken the biggest hurdle and I feel quite cheerful about the future. I am sure he will make it. Now I am wondering where we can get some kind of artificial leg.

I have been accompanying the staff on the rounds of the hospital every morning. This is an odd procedure to the uninformed. Dr. Babbar walks from bed to bed, from ward to ward, throughout the hospital, accompanied by several doctors, and trailed by an assortment of nurses, dispensers, ward servants and me. Men leap ahead of him to whisk open doors and salute as he passes. Two more carry water basins and towels in case he must wash up. Some of this retinue are necessary, the rest go along because Dr. Babbar uses this time to give the staff what is almost a refresher course in medicine. He looks at the chart of each patient, spending more time with those who are new, puzzling, or critical. The whole time he discusses various problems connected with each case, asks searching questions, suggests new treatments, and may stop in one spot for minutes at a time and lecture on some aspect of medicine or hospital routine. Dr. Babbar can be good-humored and pleasant with the staff members, but when he becomes annoyed he freezes at once—and pity the poor person who has had the ill luck to displease him!

Already, in the few weeks I have been working at the hospital, my attitude toward it has changed. It is still the same confused, untidy, primitive place, but I am seeing it with new eyes. I learn new reasons every day for the conditions which exist, and my respect is growing for the members of the hospital staff who are attempting to overcome these conditions, and help people despite them. I have stopped making mental comparisons between this hospital and the ones I know in the States, and compare only the problems with the effort being made to solve them. Dr. Babbar has been most helpful. The first two weeks that I was here I seldom saw him, and when he passed me in one of the wards, I frequently caught an expression of surprise on his face, as though he were thinking, "Is she still around? Hasn't she gone back to the bridge table yet?" My interference in the case of the man with the bad leg seems to have convinced him that I will not become easily discouraged. A day or two before the operation, Dr. Babbar sent word that I would be welcome to go on rounds with the rest of the staff, and when he suggested that I attend the amputation, I felt that I was being given a tremendous opportunity to become one of them.

At home the whole family this week has been suffering from a touch of intestinal trouble. Here this is called "Delhi Belly," and is a very common complaint among the Americans during monsoon season. We all rival each other in comparing the severity of our symptoms, and in trying to track down what it was we shouldn't have eaten. Steve and Bart are uncomfortable with heat rash, and we have been trying a variety of remedies, including a paste made from ground-up clay stone, highly recommended by Ram. Tony has such a thick skin that he only gets darker and darker with each passing day. He could easily be mistaken for an Indian.

From what we are told, the English habitually kept their children inside during the hot weather, from ten in the morning until four in the afternoon—those who did not go up to the mountains during the summer. Many times their fear of the climate even led them to send their children home alone to England at an early age. Perhaps the British, who come from a colder climate, were unable to adapt to this one, but most Americans had lived in places in the United States as hot as this, or nearly so. Here the temperature stays between ninety and one hundred and fifteen degrees during the dry season. During the monsoon it seldom goes above one hundred degrees, but the higher humidity is uncomfortable. Southern India is of course much warmer, but any talk about the misery of Indian heat in this section is a myth. Most of us permit our children to play outside all year round, and none of them seems to suffer from any ill effects. Our men work right through the heat of the day, shocking many Indians. The only Americans I have noticed concerned about the heat were those with too little to do.

Indians, in general, rich and poor, move their beds outdoors and sleep there through the summer. This gave me quite a shock when we first arrived in India. We left the airport in New Delhi late at night and made the long trip to the hotel by bus. All along the route, I could see the dim shapes of bodies lying by the roadside, their faces covered. Having read of famines in India, I thought these might be victims of starvation, lying dead and neglected. I even tried to shield the children from the horrible sight. I was amused and relieved to learn later that these were only people sleeping—and entirely alive.

Ram's war of nerves to have Jugetram made bearer has finally succeeded. He changed his tactics from concern over my "hard" work, to martyred comments about his own condition—with no bearer to help. I managed to endure the long face and mumbling from the kitchen with a good deal of enjoyment, but when I started waiting half an hour for a cup of coffee, which Ram was far too overworked to make, I made a strategic withdrawal and gave in. The coffee situation improved at once, but I soon learned that this was not the end. It seems Jugetram must now have new tailored white cotton uniforms in keeping with his new position. I demurred at this expense. Very foolish of me. I should have learned my lesson. Jugetram, who until this time has always been neatly dressed in pants and shirt, is now appearing in a tattered assortment of shreds, well calculated to stir my hard heart. I am not sure how far they will go, but I would not be surprised to have him arrive stark naked some morning, if I hold out too long.

Veteran Americans here tell us many surprising stories of unusual Indian viewpoints, but when we were told of signs posted along the railroad stating, "Please do not sleep on the tracks!" I only half believed this tall tale. Now I have met a man who must be one of the few living examples of why such warnings are posted. This man, whose name is Natu Ram, has occupied a bed in the hospital for eight months because he did, indeed, go to sleep on the tracks. He is charming, full of gracious speeches and innate courtesy. Natu speaks faltering English, and has told me about himself. He is not too clear about why he went to sleep on the tracks—he "just happened to become tired in that spot!" Yes, he had seen trains before—"very large animals." I gained the impression that he rather expected the train to step over him if it came by, rather as a horse might. Fortunately only one leg was actually on the track, and though badly damaged was saved. Natu says, "The large train came to me very fast, and threw me into the air." His attitude is one of disgust that the train should behave in this uncalled-for manner. However, I believe he will choose his bed more carefully in the future.

On Sunday we attended our first movie since leaving the United States. We have an American movie only once every two weeks, and it is shown at ten-thirty Sunday morning. This is a terrible hour to go to a show, but most of the Americans turn out anyway, since this provides almost the only familiar source of entertainment we have. The pictures are very old, and were B features to begin with, but we all sit there groaning, and enjoy them thoroughly. Frequently the operator gets the reels mixed up, and since the sequence is meaningless to him, we see the middle first, then the end and finally the beginning of the picture. This can be hilarious, as on Sunday, when the

gangster killed violently at the beginning was walking around
hale and hearty at the film's close.

I caused a crisis at home the other day. I felt very dissatisfied
with the way the new sweeper (Jugetram's wife's brother, of
course) was cleaning the toilets. Ram was told to speak to him
sharply on the subject, but no improvement was apparent. I
decided that none of the servants really understood what I
wanted. Armed with soap, scouring powder and rags, I called
them all into the bathroom to witness a demonstration. When
they were gathered there and realized what I intended to do,
they were horror-struck, and a pitched battle nearly resulted.
Jugetram pleaded with me to desist, tears in his eyes, while
Ram tried to snatch the rag from my hands. "Mem-sahibs don't
do such work," was Ram's agonized cry. In this country any
kind of work connected with latrines is done by the very lowest
of the low, and such people (formerly untouchable) even now
suffer much discrimination and shame. I did not want to give
my tacit approval to the caste system by backing down; so I
tried to explain to them that in my country such attitudes were
not known. I told them that I always cleaned my own bathrooms at home, as did everyone, and that we did not believe
there was anything disgusting about any kind of honest work.
Then I proceeded to scrub the toilet. I don't suppose any of
them really understood me. They remained utterly distressed;
Ram blushing a fiery red, and both the sweeper and Jugetram
openly crying. As I finished, Ram informed me in a disapproving voice, "My other mem-sahibs never do such a thing." I said,
"Well Ram, I do!" and left. For hours after they looked at me
sideways and stayed out of the way. I believe they think I am
subject to momentary lapses of sanity.

On the first of each month all of the peddlers in India seem
to migrate to Nangal. These men are called "wallahs" and come
from Kashmir, Delhi, and all points, carrying tremendous packs
of goods to sell. A paraphrase of an old nursery rhyme exactly
fits them: "Hark, Hark, the dogs do bark, the wallahs are com-

ing to town. Some in rags, and some in tags, and some in velvet gown." As contrasted to the everyday local peddlers, who hawk everything from chickens to peanuts, these men bring in examples of every kind of Indian craft. They have learned that the Americans here have money only on payday, so that is the day they pour into town by the dozens. For three or four days it is difficult to get a moment's peace, and if you are interested you can look from dawn to dusk at a fantastic number of varied items. Some wallahs bring delicate embroidered tablecloths and shawls from Kashmir. Others peddle jewelry—everything from crude turquoise-studded silver from Tibet to delicately enameled gold, and their pockets are filled with unset rubies and emeralds. It is lots of fun to sit on the floor, your hands filled with cut diamonds, even when you suspect they are really glass. The ivory wallahs have carved boxes and charming figures of different gods and goddesses. There are men selling brass and copper bowls and trays, and more men selling carved walnut wood.

It takes hours to look at the wares of just one man, because they all follow the same endless routine. First they enter the house, removing their shoes at the door, and supervise carefully the placing of all their packs and cases. Then after spreading a sheet over your floor, they squat down cross-legged, and start removing one item at a time from their collection and placing it on the sheet. They make a ritual of this, studying each item intently as though looking for an invisible flaw, dusting it with a dirty rag, and placing it proudly in position. You may look at these things and handle them, but the wallah will not answer any questions about price, or attempt to make a sale, until every one of his prizes is spread before you. In the case of jewelry you end up with the floor covered with piles of stones, gold rings and silver bracelets, sapphire-studded pendants and ruby earrings, and you, yourself, are a nervous wreck for fear some valuable item may roll under the couch or disappear into the baby's mouth.

When the display is set up entirely to the wallah's satisfaction the fun begins. He naturally tries to sell his most expensive items first, and does not deign to notice that you are interested in the cheaper things. All the wallahs speak English, and many keep up a constant stream of patter which would put our vacuum cleaner salesmen to shame.

"Mem-sahib, this ring I brought only for you to see. No other lady here would appreciate its great value. Only you know lovely stones. To you it is a joy to sell this priceless item."

Then I am shown a ring which contains either an enormous ruby, or the tail light from some deceased jeep. Or sad stories of old fathers and hungry children are related for my sympathy. If all else fails the wallah may pretend to be very angry with your lack of appreciation of his fine assortment and accuse you of deliberately wasting his time. Whatever the technique used, it is almost impossible to remove him from the house unless you buy some small thing. And the actual purchase may consume more hours as you bargain back and forth, and he runs the gamut of emotion from indignant surprise to tearful surrender.

Bart has no patience with any of this procedure, and a wallah never gets past the front porch when he is home. Bart got the idea, when we first arrived, that it was my intention to spend every cent of his salary on diamond bracelets and copper ash trays. He remains convinced that if I even look at someone's wares, I will succumb at once. So every night at this time of the month he enters the house after work and the first words he says are, "Ram, did mem-sahib spend too much money today?" Ram's answer depends entirely on how I stand with him at the time. When I have done what he wants, and am in favor, he says, "No, sahib, not spend money." But on bad days he assumes a worried expression, and tattles, "Oh sahib, mem-sahib spend very much money today." Then the three of us indulge in some friendly bickering: sahib pleading with Ram to restrain mem-sahib in the future, Ram shaking his head woefully at mem-sahib's extravagance, and mem-sahib loudly protesting her innocence on all charges. Ram enjoys the episode to the full, and returns to the kitchen in high good humor to relate how mem-sahib is surely driving sahib to an early grave.

six

The monsoon ended with a final shattering cloudburst. It rained almost steadily for a week, so hard that we had almost five inches in just one afternoon. The rain caused a great deal of damage at Bhakra, and severely flooded other areas. The mud houses in many nearby villages collapsed, unable to withstand the hard rain. There was little damage in Nangal since the walls of our buildings are covered with brick. Now the rains are over, and each morning and evening there is a nip in the air. The first few days that it turned cool, we wrapped up in sweaters, and lit fires. It was quite a shock when we discovered the temperature was still in the eighties. The twenty-degree drop, after being in the hundreds for so long, actually seemed chilly. Now we have become adjusted and feel merely pleasantly warm.

The most exciting event of recent weeks has been the arrival of all the goods we shipped from the States just before we left. Ram learned from one of the workmen at the railway station that our stuff had come into the freight or goods yard as they say in India. He came catapulting into the house like a whirling dervish.

"Mem-sahib, you come just now. Mem-sahib, hurry! You come to station."

I didn't have a notion what he was talking about, and his excitement and frantic pulling at my arm convinced me something terrible must have happened at the station. Finally he calmed down long enough to make himself more coherent— then I was the excited one. We were notified more officially a few minutes later, and Bart was sent home from the dam to help transport the boxes from the station to the house.

The stove and washing machine were still in the light, manufacturer's crates. Despite this they arrived without so much as a scratch, possibly because those handling them could easily see what was inside. The refrigerator, which was very heavily crated, was the most banged up, but only superficially. Everything else was in fine condition. I don't think the crates had even been opened in Indian customs. They came exactly as I had packed them; not even a phonograph record was broken.

The kids were so delighted to have their toys again that it has been just like Christmas. Steve lived in his cowboy suit for nearly a week, and Tony is still going around with his feathered headdress poking his ears out at right angles. I can certainly understand why Ram was so enthusiastic over the arrival of our belongings. Evidently the quality of our appliances has a great influence on his social position as our cook. He has polished everything to a beaming whiteness, and for two days has spent most of his time running conducted tours through our kitchen. All the servants in the neighborhood have come by to inspect *his* equipment, and compare it favorably, or otherwise, with that belonging to their own employers. I assume that we have given satisfaction, since Ram would probably have handed in his notice otherwise.

Nate is adorable these days. He is starting to say real words. For a long time he has been babbling his own secret language which has been the source of much bewilderment to the servants. He strung his nonsense syllables together with so much expression that they were all convinced he was really speaking English, and were baffled by their inability to understand him.

His very first word was "Susie," which is the name of a pet
monkey that he and Jugetram visit every morning. Nate has
developed into an artful mimic, and he loves to mimic this
monkey. He says, "Sujie, Sujie," and twists his face all up, pushing his mouth in and out, until we nearly collapse with laughter.
He also imitates our tone of voice. When we tell him, "No,"
he repeats, "No," with exactly the same inflection, then laughs
and laughs at his own cleverness.

The fact that Ram always gets his own way around the house
would not be nearly so aggravating if only he were not always
so right! The whole household has settled down—since I
capitulated on all fronts. Jugetram is doing beautifully with
the children, and the baby is his completely. With the arrival
of his new white uniforms, Jugetram's self-respect has grown
so much that he is hardly the same man. He has a naturally shy
personality, but no longer behaves with the cringing humility
I found so irritating. He is a bearer now, a person of no small
authority, in charge of mem-sahib's household and mem-sahib's
baby, and looked upon with deference by sweepers who have
not attained this eminence. Our new sweeper (whom I shall
stop calling Jugetram's wife's brother) is called Prekash. He
is a young boy, probably in his late teens, and so nearly a youngster himself that he treats our boys with an engaging lack of
formality. He scolds Steve and Tony when they make his work
more difficult, and the three of them engage in wrestling
matches on the front lawn. The peace is wonderful now that
everything has been arranged to Ram's complete satisfaction.
But I am awaiting with anticipation his next full-scale campaign.

I am spending more and more time at the hospital. Living
right next door makes running over for a few minutes a temptation. From my windows I can see the Bhakra ambulance arrive
with accident cases, or a group of villagers, carrying a homemade
stretcher, come through the gate. The hospital is so understaffed, even during light periods, that a real emergency presents

a difficult strain for everyone. Last week we had seven accident cases in one night. Three of these were skull fractures which had to be watched constantly. The same night we had a com-plicated delivery, a woman in postoperative shock, and a child brought in with peritonitis besides all the regular patients to care for. At times like these no one bothers about my lack of qualifications. I am simply put to work.

Frequently I find myself bitterly resenting our lack of various simple facilities. There is not even a hot water heater in the whole hospital. Since every bit of hot water must be heated on two electric hot plates even giving a sponge bath becomes a difficult procedure. We have about fifty link-spring hospital beds, but our few mattresses are little more than worn pads, while on many the only mattress is a folded blanket. The rest of the patients sleep on native charpoys, lying directly on the woven rope which forms their support. All these beds make the prevention of bedsores on immobilized patients nearly im-possible. Even such small items as thermometers and hypo-dermic syringes are in pitifully short supply. Medicines are carefully rationed. We have penicillin and, when used, it is given free. But hospital funds are limited, and wonder drugs are given only when all lesser remedies have failed. We cannot provide free any of the new mycin drugs. When a patient must have streptomycin or terramycin, he has to purchase it himself. The cost of these drugs makes this practically impossible for most of our patients—who simply have no money. Fortunately the Indian Red Cross and many of the Americans here contrib-ute to a fund which buys these medicines for the most needy cases.

An added strain is put on hospital resources by the Indian custom of having the whole family accompany the sick person to the hospital. At times this is an advantage. When a child is ill, one or both parents remain with him constantly, sleeping on the floor by his bed at night, sometimes for weeks at a time. Since we are too short-handed to provide the loving care a sick child needs, their presence is an asset. In the case of critically ill adults, we also encourage some relative to remain by the bed, if only to give water and assist in small ways. But the many village patients are frequently accompanied by wives, children, mothers, fathers, and even more distant relatives, who want to live on at the hospital indefinitely. They camp out in the yard, cooking small meals over open fires and wandering about in everyone's way. I particularly worry about the children who roam through the hospital by day and night, exposing themselves to all sorts of infections. Some have had one or both parents sick for months. After dark, I stumble over them curled up asleep on the cold concrete floors or on the bare ground. Many stay alive by begging their food from the already poorly nourished patients.

The very magnitude of the many problems here easily leads to a defeatist attitude. From Americans and Indians I have heard such remarks as, "What good does it do to even try, when there is so much to be done?" or, "Anything you do is such a drop in the bucket, what is the use?" and even, "Why help these people when they would all be better off dead?" People don't seem to realize that the sufferings of many are just the sufferings of one, multiplied. It is only by helping the individual that you can eventually aid the mass. And these patients of ours do not seem to realize that "they would be better off dead." They want to live as much as anyone. So, although I think a great deal about the larger problems of poverty and disease, I try to concern myself mainly with individual cases, where a little aid goes a long way, and I can do something.

Our amputation case, Bhagat Ram, is recovering slowly but surely. He does not seem displeased by the loss of his leg, and Dr. Babbar teases me, "Well, Mrs. Bartholomew, you have given India just what she needed—one more beggar!" I have been trying to find a carpenter who would be willing to take the sketches I have drawn and make a simple artificial leg. Bart did some research on prosthetic devices when we were at the

University. He can speak knowingly of suction sockets and knee joints, but all I am aiming for is a simple, lightweight peg leg. So far all the carpenters here have been afraid to attempt such a radical departure from their usual work.

Dr. Babbar has invited me to share his regular morning coffee break daily. This is very helpful, since he uses the time to tell me about welfare work he would like to see tackled, and answers my many questions about medical problems and hospital routine. I have had courses in such things as physiology and biology, but I do not know enough to be as useful here as I would like. So I am studying all Dr. Babbar's textbooks, one by one. He is much amused by my attempts to get medical education at second hand. I doubt that many doctors would be as generous as he is in giving their knowledge to an eager layman, but fortunately Dr. Babbar is a born teacher. Whenever he has some free minutes, he takes time to instruct me in something he thinks I want to know. He shows me X-ray films and teaches me how to read them by pointing out the particular signs that differentiate certain diseases. Then I practice by myself on stacks of old films, trying to decide the disease before reading the report. Recently he has had me practice handing him instruments in make-believe operations. He takes me into the operation theater, and has the instruments laid out. Then step by step he goes through every move that is made in a particular operation, explaining just what he does and what he looks for at each step, while I practice memorizing which instruments are used for which purposes, and when to give him each one. He does not like to call for his instruments, but says that he wants anyone assisting him to understand so well what is being done that the correct item is always at hand. All of this is tremendously interesting, but seems to have no end. The more I learn, the less I seem to know.

In the meantime, I still spend most of my eight hours a day with individual patients. I never lack for something to do, and among other things, I take care of the patients' personal hygiene. I am growing increasingly fond of Natu Ram, whose blithe disregard of locomotives led to disaster. He remains consistently charming, and his courteous refusal to accept any charity from me is most refreshing. I often distribute old magazines, cigarettes, fruit and so forth among the patients, but when I stop to chat with Natu Ram, he always graciously offers me something from his small hoard of possessions. Most frequently the gift is a homemade Indian cigarette, called a beede, of extreme nastiness, which I feel obliged to smoke, and still taste hours later.

I am also very attached to a little girl in the female ward. Her name is Nita, and she is suffering from an incurable and usually fatal liver disease. This ailment is characterized by the accumulation of large amounts of fluid in the abdomen, which gives the patient a strange bloated appearance. Nita is a tiny girl with a face like a hungry bird and thin claw hands. Her huge tummy makes her look oddly pregnant, and this has resulted in much teasing from the other patients. She arrived in such rags that clothes from the meager hospital stock were given her. The ugly pajama suit she now wears was meant for a grown woman, and only makes her pathetic deformity even more obvious. Every day when I enter the female wing of the hospital she is waiting for me. Never speaking, or even smiling, she silently takes my hand and goes with me from bed to bed, staying by my side until I leave again. I went to the bazaar a few days ago, and picked out some pink silk material, printed with tiny rosebuds, which a tailor is making up now. I think she should be given the chance to look pretty for a little while, and I hope to see her smile.

seven

I have heard people at home say, "We are having an old-fashioned Christmas this year." Ha! They need to be here to understand what an "old-fashioned Christmas" really means. Ours was extremely old-fashioned, and, believe me, hard work. It is all very well to talk about making your own ornaments and decorations, but try it when you can't get silver foil, or colored paper, or popcorn, or anything. All the Americans showed remarkable ingenuity. For glitter we had the mica dust they put on turbans, and ornaments were made from gold-paper garlands used for Indian weddings. We baked Christmas cookies and candy, decorated the house with cotton and homemade bells —then had a few days to admire our efforts before it was time to take the whole thing down.

Most of the Americans here get very homesick at Christmas time. And I must admit that we shared in the general longing for family and friends, but in all other ways we had a wonderful time. The Indians are all familiar with our Christmas holiday from having observed the British celebration of the day for so many years. A great many non-Christian Indians have even grown accustomed to sharing the day, and send cards and exchange presents just as we do. So in many ways the Christmas spirit was here, making the holiday more pleasant for us. The

45

children claimed, as they claim every year, that this Christmas was the best one yet.

Marshal Tito visited Nangal on the twenty-third of December. His visit kept the town in an uproar for a full two weeks. Bhakra Dam is the biggest, most impressive display of progress in India. The Indians are justifiably so proud of their efforts here that every important foreign visitor is given a guided tour of the project. To insure Tito's safety, police were imported from all over India. There were policemen stationed at every turn and by every tree and shrub. They could not quite take the place of our street-corner Santa Clauses at home, but with their bright red turbans they gave the town a festive look. We did not meet Tito. The Indians gave a lovely reception for him, but only a few Americans were invited. The Indians prefer to keep the Americans here in the background when foreign dignitaries arrive. They have a natural desire to minimize the technical assistance we are giving them, when showing off to other countries. Most of us don't mind this attitude personally, though many times we do feel we would like our work here to be more publicized for the sake of letting others know that American aid is being given. Those Americans who did meet Tito were impressed with his enormous good looks and spontaneous social grace.

I am afraid that, for most of us, Tito took a back seat to Christmas. The one thing we were all interested in was getting him out of town so that things would go back to normal. We were particularly concerned about our Christmas trees, which were on their way from the Himalayas—probably by camel back! The roads in and out of Nangal were closed, except to official traffic, for days. Besides, they were clogged to capacity with policemen stumbling over each other. We waited anxiously day after day, but no Christmas trees came. Finally, on the night of the twenty-second I decided to drive down to the bazaar and check once more. I arrived just as the trees did, so turned right around and gave a good imitation of Paul

Revere. Shouting and honking to spread the good news, I drove through the American compounds. The "trees" were really hilarious. Most were mere branches, and none had any kind of shape, but by buying two and wiring them together, we all had something that resembled a tree.

The next big event was the Christmas dance. The band belonging to the Maharajah of Patiala came to play for us. It seemed an excellent band to those of us who had been here long enough to forget American dance bands. The Indians and Americans turned out in force, and everyone behaved well and had a remarkably good time. This was the first successful venture of its kind here. Always before the dances have fallen flat, mainly because so few of the Indians dance. They attended the dances, but only to sit on the sidelines and watch us. It was disconcerting, at these affairs, to dance on a nearly empty floor watched by dozens of silent Indians. The result was that some Americans reacted with a determination to have a good time despite it, with a few too many nips at the bottle to put them in the mood. Others were too embarrassed to relax at all. But these last few months, some of the Americans have been giving informal dancing lessons to Indian friends and were nearly besieged with pupils. By the night of the dance, these students were doing a pretty fair job on the floor, and the sight of a few dancing gave many other Indians the courage to try. So it was quite a gala affair, with Indians and Americans enjoying themselves together, something that is all too rare around here.

Then came Christmas Eve. We hung seven stockings over the fireplace, three for our boys, and four for the children of the servants. Christmas morning the children were all up at four A.M. and the fun started. The five of us, the five servants and their respective families, adding up to sixteen people, gathered around the tree. It is the custom among the Americans to give all their servants some kind of gift on Christmas. But as far as I know, no one has ever shared the whole day with them, so for ours it was an exciting novelty. For each of the

men, their wives and children, I had a complete outfit of clothes
made. We also gave the adults a few small gifts, and all the
children toys, which are out of reach for most Indian children.
We all sat around the tree while Bart distributed the gifts to
each of us, one at a time. For me, the greatest pleasure of Christmas was watching the servants and their delight. Jugetram's
bewitching daughter, Bimela, is four, but no larger than our
baby. She unwrapped her doll first, and then could not bear to
lay it down and unwrap anything else. Ram's daughter, Rani,
is eight, and very sweet and shy. She was so overwhelmed that
she did not even want to open the packages, but held them
tightly, touching the ribbon and paper gently, her eyes like stars.
The two little boys, Saudi and Kushour, were younger and less
awed, and soon joined our children in pushing toy cars all over
the floor.

The day was not without its disappointments. I had my heart
set on getting a horse. I even had him picked out, the obviously
intelligent beast who pulls the coal wagon. Bart considered this
one of my wackier notions, and would not listen to reason at
all. However, the servants have more sympathy for my ideas,
and they presented me with a pair of ducks and a little billy
goat. Bart says he is going to tack up a sign, "Nangal Zoo," if
I go ahead with my plans to add a donkey and baby camel to
the pet menagerie. Most of the animals here are pathetic. Poor
breeding and not enough food make them scrawny and unattractive. The goats are an exception. The adults are lovely agile
animals, and the babies wobbly and adorable. It is difficult to
keep pets here because of the marauding jackals and hyenas
that roam our yards at night and attack any small animal. My
solution of this problem has Bart tearing out his hair in chunks.
Ram and I put the ducks to sleep in the washroom, under the
overturned clothes basket. But the goat presented a graver
challenge, which we met in a way we hoped to keep secret.
Unfortunately Bart spoiled it all that night by going into the
kitchen for a glass of water. When he stumbled into the goat

tied to the kitchen table the roof nearly went off the house. For once Ram and I were united in a common cause. Luckily for me, the *Saturday Evening Post* had arrived with a very complimentary article about goats. But Bart maintains that every time I want to do some crazy thing I can locate a fool who advocates it.

Christmas has turned our thoughts to the trip home, even though this is far in the future. And I am in trouble over that too. I explained to the family my idea of the right way to go —by camel caravan to the coast then by Arab dhow to Africa. This itinerary was greeted with grim silence by Bart, but the children are enthusiastic. They are making his life miserable with, "But daddy, why can't we go on camels? But why not?" With two more years to work on him, I haven't given up yet. Someone is certain to come to my assistance by writing "On Camel Back Through India."

We had a program and party for the younger children the day before Christmas. One of the fathers, looking very sheepish in a homemade Santa Claus suit, distributed small gifts. Afterward all the school children took a decorated tree up to the children's ward at the hospital. They also passed around oranges and candy to the patients, and wished everyone a Merry Christmas with so much vigor that we were extremely glad there was no one seriously ill. On Christmas Eve the teen-agers went up to the hospital to sing carols. The patients enjoyed this custom very much. The whole hospital listened quietly as the children moved from ward to ward singing all our old favorites in their clear young voices.

On Christmas day many of the tradespeople come around for a small tip or, as it is called here, "baksheesh." This means we give money, candy or fruit, and in return receive leis of flowers, called garlands, to put round our necks. Poor Bart was nearly driven crazy by people dropping in from the hospital. Many brought us flowers, but most of them were just curious and wanted to see the tree and the lights. They would come in salaaming, squat on the floor and talk to us in Punjabi while I passed cookies. After ten minutes or so they would get up and file out and more would arrive. It made Bart uncomfortable. "But what do they want?" he kept mumbling, or, "Carol, are you sure *that* is not contagious?" Bart is really getting very jumpy. The other day I merely mentioned that I had met a very interesting woman from South India, who had started a leper colony single-handed. Before I was even finished, he ran out of the room shouting, "No! No! I simply won't have it."

So this has been our Christmas. We have had the usual Santa Claus and trees, the tinsel and songs, but my thoughts all through the holiday kept turning to the fact that we were honoring an event that must have taken place in a village not very different from this one. In all the hundreds of years that have passed these people and this place have remained almost unchanged. To Him whose birth we were remembering, this way of life, not our own, would be familiar. And Americans who profess to find the Indians primitive, ignorant and dirty, forget that Jesus was one with people like these. Buried here in this far-off spot, our civilization seems impossibly remote and rather insignificant. We remember the shiny abundance of life in America, as our children will remember this Christmas. But it is this way of life that seems most permanent and timeless. One feels that after we have playfully blown up the glittering façade of our material advancement, this civilization will go on. People here will till their fields, water their animals and probably never notice that we are gone.

eight

Christmas is over, and we have settled back to normal. Life here is far from being all work and no play. Despite Bart's long hours on the dam, and mine at the hospital, we have more leisure together than we had at home—thanks to Ram and his cohorts. The Americans here enjoy an active social life. We all go out more in the evenings than we would ordinarily because we have the servants to act as built-in baby sitters at no extra cost. This is like a miracle to many of us who were almost housebound in the States. Then, also, there is really so little here in the way of passive entertainment. With no television, poor radio reception, no restaurants or soda fountains, only one movie every two weeks, and even a lack of books and magazines, we are thrown on our own resources.

The principal recreation for most of us is playing cards, either bridge or canasta. A game called Scrabble has been brought over from the States by some of the new arrivals, and it is popular among the women. We also get together for pot-luck dinners, and frequently someone will give an informal party with records and dancing. Since winter has arrived many of the women are gathering at one house to knit together. We try to supplement our husbands' wool socks since American men (and women) have enormous feet by Indian standards, and it is

51

difficult to find footwear large enough. The Indian women put us all to shame with their knitting. Their hands move like quicksilver and they never need to look at what they are doing. I am a hopeless knitter and spend most of my time waiting for someone to pick up dropped stitches and untangle the mess I have made. I feel very incompetent when I see little Indian girls knitting away using only two rough twigs and bits of string.

The degree to which we share our social life with the Indians depends entirely on the individual American family. Some of the Americans mix very little with the Indians, others entertain Indian friends frequently. On the whole, the women mix much more, socially, than the men. We enjoy frequent luncheons together, and many of the women, Indian and American, have formed cooking classes where we teach each other our national dishes. There is one very simple reason which partly explains why we do not enjoy evenings together more often, the difference in our dinner hours. It seems absurd, until you try to get around it. Our husbands work actively outside all day, and it is the custom among construction families to have an early dinner, almost as soon as the men come home. Then we spend the early evening with the children, reading to them and putting them to bed. Not until around eight o'clock do we have guests or go out. Contrasted to this, the Indian routine is to have an English tea at five o'clock or so, then enjoy their social life, returning home for dinner between eight-thirty and ten o'clock, and retiring immediately thereafter.

If we share the Indian tea and put off our dinners until later, our husbands groan and moan about drinking cups of tea when they want meat and potatoes, and the children miss out on their customary dinner with us and playtime afterward. If we have Indian guests for dinner, they arrive about seven, we eat at eight, and by nine they are ready to leave, when for us the evening has just begun. It seems to be Indian courtesy to leave very shortly after dinner, but it is disappointing when they depart just as we are starting to enjoy ourselves. The Indian schedule for meals probably worked well socially during the days of English rule, but the conflict with American custom is very difficult, and neither group seems able to find a satisfactory mutual compromise.

Of course there are many other reasons why Indians and Americans do not enjoy each other more and are not better friends. Some of these reasons are actually insignificant, such as the habit some Indians have of talking past us in Hindi, when they are well able to speak English. I don't mind this at all, because I can understand how easy it must be for them to drop unthinkingly into their native language. In fact, it is we who should learn their tongue. But this slip by an educated Indian is felt by some Americans to be deliberate rudeness.

Other reasons are not so petty. Indian class distinctions are very distasteful to most Americans. Our attempts to be on friendly, informal terms with the many "low-class" Indian foremen and technicians who work closely with our husbands at Bhakra are misunderstood and criticized by the "upper-class" Indian engineers with whom we are expected to mix. Many of us have endured embarrassing incidents when an Indian engineer has arrived unexpectedly, only to find us entertaining "mere workmen." The calculated rudeness of the upper-class Indian toward our poor guests on these occasions has antagonized many of us. So some Americans confine all their social contacts to these so called "lower classes," since it seems impossible to mix with both groups, and they prefer to find friends among the many intelligent workers.

Another barrier to our mixing more freely is the subtle pressure put on most Americans by their servants. None of our servants seem to want us to entertain Indian guests, and they make it difficult for us to do so in innumerable small ways. When I tell Ram we are going to have company for dinner, he always asks, "Indian or American?" If I say American, all goes well and he outdoes himself to prepare a meal that will do him credit. On the evening in question, he passes drinks in a spotless uniform, smiling and proud. No matter how late our guests stay, or how much work there is to do, he seems to enjoy the party as much as we do. But what a difference when our guests are Indians! Then for days his head aches, his feet hurt, and he is sadly overworked. The dinner he cooks is poor, and only my constant prodding ensures that it is even adequate. He appears, sullen-faced, in a dingy uniform, to serve drinks or wait at table, and slams dishes and pans around in the kitchen with an excess of noise. Many of the other Americans tell me that they endure the same sort of passive resistance from their cooks, so it is not just Ram.

I can only believe that, among the lower classes here, there exists a deep resentment and dislike for the upper classes, who have so much more than they. The odd part is that high-class Indians do not seem to be aware of how much they are hated by the vast majority of their underprivileged. In classing this tremendous group as inferior and keeping them always at a subservient distance, the upper classes have lost the opportunity to learn what the lower-class individuals are actually like. Some of them do not know their own people as well as we do, because they cannot really believe there is anything worth knowing. Americans have frequently been stunned by the ignorance of educated Indians regarding underprivileged Indians. Many Indian engineers are unaware that some of their workmen speak excellent English, nor can they admit that many of these men are intelligent and sensible, despite a lack of formal education. Indeed, the most thoughtful statements regarding Indian problems and possible solutions have been made to us by these uneducated men, not by their social superiors.

I have deliberately refrained from speaking of caste prejudice until now, because it has been impossible for me to decide how much of the snobbery we find here is the result of centuries of the caste system, and how much is simply due to a society based on classes, similar to that of the English. The Indians themselves tell me that caste was never so rigid in Northern India as it still is farther south, and this appears to be true. Certainly I have never observed the kind of vicious treatment of low castes that is written about so frequently in books. I may be quite mistaken in feeling that here it is as much class as caste, but it doesn't really matter since the results are much the same.

No American can fully appreciate how truly classless our country is until he lives in another where such distinctions are an integral part of everyone's life. It is embarrassing and difficult for us even to think in terms of "upper" and "lower" classes. I find myself hesitating each time I type the words. But it would be ridiculous to ignore the fact that these distinctions exist in India. And the fact that they exist makes getting along with Indians a difficult procedure. If we choose to adopt certain Indian attitudes and mix only with educated Indians, we alienate a much larger group. On the other hand, if we mix only with the less privileged classes, the educated Indian feels we must, ourselves, be inferior. It is not easy to walk a tightrope between the classes, keeping the good will of both. I think it is most unfortunate that American dealings with India, on the diplomatic and political level, are necessarily so exclusively with well-born government intellectuals. If these men are as misled about their own people as the educated group here, they must in turn be misleading us.

Bart is finding his work extremely challenging. He is in charge of erecting the four-mile-long conveyor belt line which will deliver rock aggregate and sand to the dam site, to be mixed with cement, for the making of concrete. In order to put up the belt, with its towers and tunnels, he has had to do a lot of preliminary work, such as blasting roads through the mountains to gain access to the belt line site. He attempted the first blast in the daytime, with humorous results. He and his men wired all the charges, everyone ran for cover, and just as Bart prepared to set off the blast, he looked up. A whole herd of goats was wandering down the mountainside, tripping over wires and stumbling into dynamite holes. The poor farmer in charge of the animals could not understand what all the excitement was about. It took the men hours to chase off the last stray goat and reset all the explosives. Now Bart does most of his blasting at night when there are fewer people around and consequently less danger.

I have driven out to Bhakra with Bart several times when he had to do some night blasting. This is not my idea of how to spend a pleasant evening, but it certainly has its exciting moments. Last night we drove out again, about eight o'clock. Now that winter has come it is completely dark at this time, and the ride to the dam site is very lonely. There was no other traffic on the winding road except for a few villagers trudging home, stacks of firewood balanced on their heads. Swinging around turns, our lights picked up the reflection of green eyes from the many cows and goats clustered about small water holes, and occasionally a glow of cigarettes told us that some tired farmers were sharing an evening smoke by the side of the road. It never fails to startle me when our quiet journey through the dark countryside carries us so suddenly into the midst of the bright lights and activity of the work site.

We drove downriver from Bhakra, then jolted and bounced up the dirt road Bart is building. The road ended abruptly at a small hill, our blast job for the night. As we stopped the pick-up and got out to stretch, the shadows around us came alive, and the foreman and workers who had remained on duty to safe-guard the charges gathered for their orders. Bart had told me that these men had gone without their dinners to stay behind at the day shift's end, so we packed a lunch for them of fruit, sandwiches and hot tea. Americans commonly show this kind of consideration to the men with whom they work. Indian laborers (or coolies, as they are called here) are so unused to being treated as human beings that these small acts make a deep impression, and are one of the reasons why the Indian workmen would rather work for American bosses than Indian. Bart introduced me to each man (something else an Indian boss would not do), then we settled for a picnic by the lights of the pickup. The hot tea tasted good even to me, and I was warmly dressed. Some of the men were shivering uncontrollably, clutching ragged shawls about them to cover their thin cotton shirts.

I passed around cigarettes, and we all had a smoke, while Bart made a last-minute check of the wiring and charges. Then we were ready to go, piling together into the pickup and jolting back to the junction of the main road. Bart left me inside the cab with dire warnings not to get out until he returned. The men scattered down the road in either direction to wave red flags and hold back traffic. Bart ran back up the new road to set off the blast, and I could hear him shouting to the lookouts for an all clear. Their voices drifted back one by one, then there was a long moment of complete silence. The whole mountain erupted in front of my eyes with a noise like a giant firecracker, and rocks and dirt blew up in every direction. At the height of the explosion, the power lines were smashed together, and we were treated to an unexpected show of vivid blue and green flashes, which put out every light in the area. I was left huddled in blackness, with visions of Bart wrapped in live wires somewhere under the debris. It seemed a very long time before he came back to the truck, and when he gleefully announced, "Boy oh boy, that was a good one," I could have hit him over the head!

We have had several interesting cases at the hospital in the past few weeks. One of these was a five-year-old girl, badly burned. When her father carried her in, the burns were already four days old. Because of heavy winter rains, the river had cut off their village and left them stranded until the water went down. When I saw them, the child was lying in the dirt in front of the hospital while her mother crouched over her crying. Various minor members of the hospital staff were passing by within a few feet of the pair, but not one of them made any attempt to direct them to a doctor or to get the child admitted. I was furious, and even more so when I had taken the girl's temperature and found it to be a hundred and four degrees. Things moved at their usual Indian pace, while one person went to fill out admission papers, another to see if a bed was free, and someone else to find a doctor. My own ignorance led me to be more upset than was probably justified by their slowness. To me, the baby looked completely charred. There was not an inch of her skin that was not crusted and black. Her limpness and feeble whimpers frightened me terribly. I learned later, when we had cleaned her up and dressed the burns, that most of this charred appearance was caused by a thick layer of soot and charcoal mixed with urine, which had been plastered over the burns four days before. But at the time I thought she must be in horrible pain and in danger of dying if we didn't work quickly.

After storming in my bastard Punjabi at every staff member in sight, with little or no effect, I invaded Dr. Babbar's office and dragged him out to see the case. When Dr. Babbar appears, it automatically lights a fire under everyone in the hospital, a fact I find very useful but hate to rely on, since running to him antagonizes the staff members. I detest being a tattletale, but I detest even more knowing that a patient is not being properly cared for. Soon after Dr. Babbar arrived on the scene, the little girl was in the emergency room, given sedation, penicillin, cleaned up and finally put to bed. She is doing very well, and will probably not even be scarred.

Another case was really a tremendous joke on me. Early on the morning after the burned child arrived, I went over to the hospital to check on her condition. When I entered the corridor, by the still deserted offices, I found a man groaning in agony on the floor. I concluded at once that here was another emergency case being overlooked and neglected. I knelt down beside the man, who was little more than a writhing bundle of rags, and asked him, in my very feeble attempts with the language, "What is wrong? Where do you feel pain?" As I reached out to take his pulse, he sat up and answered me, in perfect Oxford English, "Madam," he said, "I am suffering quite dreadfully from piles!"

nine

Life here is very peaceful and very good. No small reason for this is the slow pace at which even the least activity moves. Most Indians have little sense of urgency about anything, which is certainly not the American temperament. Those of us who try to fight this leisurely approach to life only end up frustrated and in a constant turmoil. Personally, while this inability to feel any pressure or to hurry for any reason frequently irritates me at the hospital, at other times I find it delightful and amusing; though it is true that one never seems to get even small things accomplished. For instance, it takes me nearly an hour to mail a letter.

Our post office is only a block away, but it is when I arrive that the fun begins. Although I would just as soon mail my letter and depart, this is impossible. First of all I must not be allowed to stand in line outside the building like a commoner, so the beaming clerks bow me in and with great ceremony lead me to a chair—not just any chair, but the best in the office. Since I am much too important to be waited on by a mere clerk, the postmaster himself must attend to me. If the postmaster is otherwise occupied, I wait quietly until he hurriedly finishes his business and turns to me. Then he politely asks about my family and I inquire just as politely about his. We discuss his brother-in-law's sister's coming operation in detail. Soon my postmaster is crushed by the realization that I have remained in his office unrefreshed. Stern and urgent orders are issued for ice water to be brought, which means that some poor man must go chasing out to the bazaar for ice. While waiting for my drink, we continue our conversation, discussing the weather, the great nobility of my character, the great nobility of *his* character and other inspirational topics. The ice comes; the glass is wiped with a dirty rag so that I can see how clean they are being, and I drink my water. After thirty minutes of this kind of formality, my host finally inquires, "May I assist you in any way?" I point to the letter which has been lying directly before his eyes the whole time, and say, "I would like to mail this letter."

Ah! Such action, such whizzing efficiency! A boy is dispatched to bring the scales, someone else is sent to find the stamps. Oh, dear, the letter is very heavy. Apologies are made to me for the amount I will have to pay. The letter is weighed again, on different scales. Alas, it is still heavy. I explain that it also contains snapshots. Everyone nods wisely. Indeed, it is well known that these increase weight. We become involved in a discussion of cameras which threatens to continue all day. Finally I make a move, the letter is stamped, my change returned, and I am ceremoniously escorted out. I leave thoroughly entranced by the whole episode. However, the same sort of routine occurs constantly over the simplest things and drives many Americans nearly to distraction.

At the hospital, I have been helping out more and more in the operation theater, and find surgery continually fascinating. The poverty of the rest of the hospital extends to the theater. Our doctors' coats are patched and mended, and the operating gowns look as though they have had acid thrown on them. We have a shortage of rubber gloves and instruments, so that we frequently have to wait while these are hurriedly resterilized between operations. Perhaps worst of all is the quality of our catgut. We are still using the stock left behind by the American Army in 1945, nearly sixty per cent of which has deteriorated to uselessness. It is agonizing to watch Dr. Babbar doing major surgery on a patient in critical condition, and to see almost every stitch pulled tight, only to break and have to be retied. Last week he did a hysterectomy on a woman whose hemoglobin was in the fifties. In the middle of the operation, the gut broke five times while he was trying to tie an artery. Finally, Dr. Babbar looked directly at me and said, "God damn you Americans, leaving us all your rotten gut!" There was a long moment of silence. Then I laughed and made a rather earthy joke about it. The tension was relieved and everyone else laughed too—but I understood how Dr. Babbar felt.

Working here, I do not think of myself as an American surrounded by alien people. Both the hospital and the patients have become "mine." I frequently find myself thinking of our hospitals at home with a passionate jealousy and hatred. How dare they have so much when we have so little? "They" have X-ray machines that are not held together with wire, and work more than one day in three; beautiful clean sheets, changed every day; comfortable beds, and towels, and ice water; and more than anything else, beautiful diet kitchens filled with lovely, nourishing food! When you see so many people suffering for lack of so many things, your inclination is to feel not gratitude for that which you are given, but resentment that you cannot have all you so desperately need. I well understand now why American aid is not always as appreciated as we think it should be. After all, aid is weighed in the receiver's mind against what the giver has—and what the receiver has not. If the aid given is like two dried beans in a soup pot of need and the giver does not appear to have reduced his wealth one iota by giving, it is hard to feel any great gratitude. And there is no use trying to convince anyone that we *have* deprived ourselves by giving. One can speak about the national debt and higher taxes, but they see only our standard of living, undiminished in its richness.

Little Nita, the child with ascites, has left the hospital. I feel almost to blame for getting her the new clothes. When her pink silk pajama suit arrived, it made quite a hit, not only with Nita, but with her mother and the other patients. I got her all dressed up in it, combed her hair, and even tied her pigtails with pink ribbons. She looked very sweet, like a fragile, painted sparrow. She behaved more like a shy peacock, and pranced delicately through the hospital—for once at least the object of admiring eyes. We were all pleased by her obvious pleasure, and then the blow fell. Her mother insisted on removing her from the hospital back to her village. She said there was a wedding they must attend, but I feel certain she would have left Nita behind if it had not been for the new clothes. I feel that she only wanted to show off her sudden good fortune to the villagers. We pleaded, threatened and cajoled to no avail. In the time Nita has been here, we have treated her hookworm, anemia and malaria, slowly building up her general health. Now all our efforts will be for nothing, since she will certainly deteriorate quickly through neglect. Dr. Babbar says that she will probably die in the village within a month or so. Nita and I cried when I kissed her goodbye, and I can not help feeling that I shortened her life when I bought her that silk.

I have been spending some time with another girl, the one with the missing cheek, no longer missing since Dr. Babbar closed it with plastic surgery a few weeks ago. She was suffering from a disease called cancrum oris, which was finally brought under control. Now she is not nearly so disfigured, although her face will always be scarred. Our present problem is to work the stiffness out of her jaw, which has been immobilized for a long time. Right now she can only open her mouth enough to drink fluids, and my job is to force her jaw to open a bit wider every day. This is an ordeal I detest, and I am not doing very

well. I am so afraid of hurting her that I lose my nerve. Dr.
Babbar is getting thoroughly disgusted with me.

In fact Dr. Babbar has finally started scolding me in front of
the rest of the staff, which is very gratifying though hardly enjoyable. Until recently he has been unfailingly polite and rather
formal, helping me immeasurably, and correcting me privately
whenever I stepped out of line. Now I must beware! On rounds
I hear, "Mrs. Bartholomew, I thought I asked you to take care
of this," or "Mrs. Bartholomew, why haven't you seen to that?"
Now I feel that slowly he and the rest of the staff are beginning
to forget that I am an outsider, and to treat me as one of themselves. I know I can never belong entirely, but I would like to
be taken for granted.

I have been in hot water lately over one particular patient.
This man, named Pritam Singh, was brought to the hospital
about three weeks ago. He belongs to a militant sect of Sikhs
called Akalis. This group of Sikhs are fanatically religious, and
still hold to the old forms of dress and customs. Pritam was
brought to the hospital by two relatives, an old man and a boy.
His arrival caused quite a stir, since all three were decked in
full regalia. They each wore vivid blue turbans decorated with
medallions; in their belts were stuffed knives and a sword, and
the two healthy ones carried pikestaves. Pritam was far from
healthy. He had been thrown from a horse several days before,
and had remained semiconscious ever since. All Sikhs have a
religious prohibition against ever cutting any of their hair, and
Pritam looked like a wounded Samson. His turban was set
askew on top of his uncombed mane which hung nearly to his
hips in thick black waves. His beard was equally untamed and
long, giving the poor man, even in his condition, a ferocious
appearance. In his coma he kept one hand tight around his
knife handle, which, along with the suspicious scowls of his
cohorts, was hardly reassuring. We X-rayed him, removed part
of his arsenal, and put him to bed, our every move fiercely
watched by his companions.

The X-ray revealed a severe skull fracture. We did what we could, but he lapsed into unconsciousness for nearly two weeks. His magnificent body and tangled hair made him look like a sleeping giant. The two watchdogs stayed constantly by his side, feeding him sips of gruel and bathing his face. As Pritam regained consciousness, their faithful service was poorly rewarded. At the first sign of his friend's improvement, the old man returned to the village, but the boy remained. Two days later Pritam flung himself out of bed, snatched his knife and attacked the youngster. Only Pritam's weakened condition, and the boy's agility prevented a very bloody murder. The boy also left after this episode, and we have had to deal with the raving Pritam alone. He has continued to be more and more violent, shouting abuse at nurses and patients, and threshing about his bed continually. We have been forced to tie his wrists and ankles, which has enraged him even more.

Indians seem to have rather a medieval attitude toward mental disturbances, and the hospital staff infuriates me by finding Pritam's antics amusing. They find my behavior toward him even more humorous, although they are not inclined to adopt it. I sit by Pritam's side, hold his hand and talk to him. I know he cannot understand a word I say, but he usually quiets down and watches me. He is probably only wishing he could get to his knife and shut me up. However, I keep thinking of how it must seem to him to wake up tied to a bed in a strange place, surrounded by unknown faces, and with a painfully confused head. I hope that my occasional presence and interest register somewhere in his brain, and reassure him slightly.

But none of this is the reason I am in trouble. The source of difficulty for me is Pritam's hair. I am supposed to be in charge of getting the patients to keep clean and tidy: bathing them when necessary, combing their hair, seeing to it that they clean their mouths, and so forth. And Pritam's head and beard have me completely beaten. All the time that he was unconscious we did not disturb him any more than necessary. So his hair

went untouched, becoming more and more matted as he tossed
and turned on his bed. Now he is a complete mess. His waist-
long beard and hip-long hair are tangled and snarled into matted
hunks. Lint, bits of leaves, even dried blood are ensnarled in
each lock, until he looks like a male Medusa. And every day I
hear the same refrain from Dr. Babbar. "This patient is a dis-
grace to our whole hospital. His head is filthy. Who is in charge
of hygiene in this ward?" I know very well that Dr. Babbar is
quite aware that I am, but I meekly reply. "Well, Mrs. Bartholomew, when are you going to do something about this man's
hair?" he inquires sarcastically. To which I can make no answer. I suspect that he is mainly teasing me, since he knows
Pritam's insane condition and understands that we cannot cut
a single hair for religious reasons. I cannot comb the mess without first washing it, and I cannot wash it while he is threshing
around tied to his bed.

The whole thing is getting out of hand. The rest of the staff
are delighted at my discomfiture, for which I don't blame
them, but it is becoming increasingly a matter of pride. If I
don't find some means of dealing with Pritam's hair soon, I will
lose face with everyone, and my position here will suffer accord-
ingly.

There is so much beauty here that it sometimes pulls the
tears to my eyes. I don't know whether I love it because it is so
beautiful, or if it only seems beautiful because I love it so. There
is a pinch in my heart every time I look around me and realize
that I cannot have all this forever. The temporary nature of my
stay makes every day more vivid and precious to me. It is the
end of winter now, and all day long the sun shines through a
clear blue sky. Inside our houses it is cold and damp, since the
thick mud walls hold the night chill. But outside the air is
brisk and fresh, laced with the drifting smoke from countless
tiny fires. Sometimes the stillness is so complete that I can hear

people calling back and forth in the villages across the river.

Yesterday I decided to go for a walk along the river bank. The water is low and sand bars on either side nearly meet. Women washing clothes on the rocks smiled and greeted me as I passed, and some of the children grabbed my hands and chased along beside me. I met the two daughters of an Indian friend of mine, and they walked along with me chattering about their school-work. The girls are Sikhs and were going to visit their guru, much as we might pay a call on our minister. They invited me to come along, assuring me that it would be quite all right. We climbed up a narrow path at the water's edge to a small white temple under a tremendous mango tree. The three of us slipped out of our shoes at the entrance so that no leather would profane the temple, and the girls called out to the guru, who was sitting motionless inside.

While it is true that India suffers from hordes of roving holy men whose sincerity is open to question, there are many genuine sadus and gurus who live lives of poverty and prayer, serving as religious guides and teachers to their people. This man was such a one, a Sikh guru who lived in the tiny temple compound, practicing and preaching his religion. I gave him the Sikh greeting, which sounds like, "Sat-sri-akal," but we could not talk at all. I studied him tactfully while the two girls explained who I was and paid their respects. He smiled at me frequently, and I smiled back with the feeling that we were sharing our pleasure in the youth and enthusiasm of the children. He was a lovely old man with a crisp white beard and wonderfully sweet child's eyes. I would have been glad to sit under the mango for a long time, watching the three of them, but the girls had to go. As we rose to leave, the guru went into the temple and returned with a small pot of some whitish mixture. This he scooped up with his fingers, and gave some to each of us. From the pleased looks of the girls, I suspected that this reward was one reason for their visit, and from the guru's twinkle, I think he suspected it too. We walked home along the road, the two youngsters eating their treat and I sampling mine. I think it was made from sugar and buffalo milk boiled thick, but it was too sticky for me. I ate it anyway, with what enthusiasm I could muster, not certain what heresy I might commit by throwing it away.

ten

Well, I have washed Pritam's hair! I woke up the other morning filled with resolution and resolve, and decided to do the job while my nerve held. I collected shampoo, towels and a comb from our house and marched to the hospital. There I informed Prem, a ward boy, and Prekash, one of the sweepers, of my intention, and requested a bucket of hot water. I made all my preparations near a bench in the inner courtyard, feeling that, if I was going to be slaughtered, it would not do to disturb the other patients. I told my two helpers to keep everyone away from me, and Prem indicated that he would stay out of sight, nearby. Prekash wrung his hands mournfully, and muttered, "Oh, Mem-sahib, very big man, very bad, oh, Mem-sahib!" Still I could not help feeling that he had a glint of anticipation in his eyes.

Finally the water was ready and so was I. I went to the ward to untie Pritam, and everyone scattered to watch from a safe distance. I would not have been nearly so concerned over the whole business if Pritam's hair had not been fraught with religious significance. Under ordinary circumstances it is far from tactful even to comment on the beard and hair of the Sikh, and I was quite certain that for a young Christian female to wash them must be a radical innovation. I sat down beside Pritam and tried to explain what I was going to do, using gestures, and the Punjabi words for "wash" and "hair." I kept talking to him, in what I hoped was a soothing manner, while I untied his ankles, and then his wrists. As soon as one hand was free I gave him a towel to hold, then taking his other hand I led him out to the courtyard and the scrubbing began. Nothing happened at all. We both got soaking wet, and Pritam never lost his expression of puzzlement, but that was all. After the shampoo, I started to comb a strand at a time, and found it a nearly hopeless project. When it became obvious that no blood was to be shed, some of the ward boys came out of concealment and helped me comb. We kept up a conversation with Pritam, telling him how wonderful he looked, and that soon he would once again be wearing a turban. After an hour and a half, I left to change clothes, while Prem and Prekash continued the job. Three hours later we were finished. There were still huge knotted hunks no comb would penetrate, but we managed to oil and wind it into a neat semblance of topknot. Pritam went back to bed, meek as a lamb, but he would not give up his towel, and at this moment is still clutching it.

I do not know what the Indians think about my behavior in the hospital. I do so many things that no Indian woman would consider proper that I think my conduct with the male patients sometimes comes under suspicion. Here the work that nurses do is mainly limited to giving medicines, injections, taking temperatures, and so forth. They do none of the bedpan labor, nor do they bathe male patients, prepare them for operations, or indeed have any contact with them beyond what is absolutely necessary. For me, on the other hand, the male patients are much the easiest to work with, primarily because most of them speak at least a little English. Most of the women patients speak no English, are extremely shy, and my presence embarrasses them almost as much as that of a man might. The women usually spend a relatively short time in the hospital, while on the male side we have many accident cases from the dam who must remain sometimes for months. So I spend much of my time with the male cases, who, I consider, have more need of the services of a social worker. I make a complete fool of myself in order to get some of them to laugh: cracking hard-boiled eggs on their heads, making faces, pulling their noses, mocking them when they are morose and continually sacrificing dignity to fight apathy. When you cannot really talk to people as you would like, or comfort them with words, it becomes almost instinctive to reach out a hand in the hope that your touch will convey your concern. So I pat shoulders, stroke foreheads, and sometimes sit by the side of a patient in pain holding his hand. Our patients would be astounded, to say the least, if an Indian lady should behave in this fashion, and I can hardly imagine myself duplicating this behavior in one of our own hospitals, but here I am neither fish nor fowl. I don't believe these patients think of me as a nurse, or even as a woman, but rather as a white mem-sahib—a nebulous, all-powerful figure.

This instinct to make some physical gesture of comfort seems to be in direct proportion to the misery of the patient. The more dirty and physically disgusting the illness, the more I feel compelled to demonstrate that I feel no revulsion. This tendency gets me into trouble with Dr. Babbar, who gives me stern warnings about contagion, and even threatens to bar me from the operating theater if I handle a particularly infectious case. I spend all day scrubbing my hands and running home to change clothes, but still I forget.

Yesterday I came upon a woman crouched in the courtyard of the hospital, sobbing. She was completely concealed in a pajama suit, with her scarf pulled down, hiding her face. I assumed this to be from modesty, not uncommon in village women. I knelt down beside her, and put my arm around her shoulder, beckoning for one of the walking patients to translate her words. "Mem-sahib, she is a very sick woman," he told me, "and none of the doctors will give her any treatment." I made soothing noises, at which she cried all the more loudly and tried to kiss my feet. I decided to take her to Dr. Babbar, and at least find out the truth of her complaint. I suspected she might have tuberculosis, which we do not treat. T.B. of the lungs is so widespread we would have room for no other cases if we admitted these, and the contagious aspects of the disease and the expensive nature of the treatment further prohibit us. But I thought someone could explain to her what she should do, and encourage her to try to get into one of the overcrowded T.B. hospitals. So I pulled her to her feet and led her to the doctor's office while she clung to me, her head buried on my shoulder, still sobbing. When I entered Dr. Babbar's room, he gave us one shocked look, and even forgot himself and used my first name. "Good God, Carol," he shouted, "get away from that woman!" I was so surprised by his reaction that I pulled away without thinking, and made my feeble plea, "Doctor, she is terribly upset. What is wrong?" "Have you looked at her?" he asked. When I shook my head, he told the woman to slip out of her ragged jacket and drop her scarf. I won't describe what I saw, but it was quite a shock. "What is it?" I asked. "I am not certain, I have not had much experience with skin diseases but most likely leprosy," he replied sternly. "Anyway we can't treat her here!" The woman dressed again, and he explained to her where she must go to be treated, a hospital a hundred miles away. I followed her outside to give her some money for the train fare, and when she finally stumbled away, I realized that once again my arm had been around her shoulder. Leprosy is not really very contagious, but I went home and bathed.

After many months I finally have an artificial leg for Bhagat Ram. A burly Sikh carpenter turned up one day and assured me that he would make the leg for one hundred rupees (about twenty dollars). I gave him some sketches and showed him how to measure Bhagat's stump, and he went away. I was certain it would be just another false alarm. After six weeks, when I had almost forgotten the incident, he appeared again with the

finished leg. Bhagat Ram has been well for some time, although
we are still treating his anemia and struggling to get rid of his
hookworm. Dr. Babbar has permitted him to live in a shed
near the hospital, mostly for my sake, since he knows how eager
I was to get him some sort of leg before he left for his village.
Well, I wish I could say that Bhagat Ram greeted the leg with
tears in his eyes, but this is far from the truth. It took literally
hours for us to talk him into even trying it. I was amazed at how
well our carpenter had done with no experience. The most I
had hoped for was a simple peg leg, but he had managed to
make one with a movable knee that bends for sitting, and locks
tight in a straight position. Even the socket was almost perfect.
I knitted a stump sock for Bhagat, and took the leg over to
him feeling the patient was getting everything it was in our
power to give him. Bhagat took one look at that leg, and his
face was a picture of mulish obstinacy. He would not even try
it on. Somehow he had found out how much the carpenter
had charged me to make it. He felt the amount was excessive,
and that I had been cheated. He was angry that I had not simply
given him the money. I am sure he would not have used the
hundred rupees to get himself a leg, nor do I believe he could
ever have got a better one for the same amount. I was so angry
I would gladly have hit him over the head with the leg. Finally
I insisted that he come over to our bungalow and talk to Bart
and the carpenter about the leg and let us show him how to use
it. He agreed to do this and I asked one of the doctors to come
also and help us persuade him. The four of us spent three hours
arguing, threatening, pleading, while Bhagat Ram sat in stub-
born silence. At last he seemed to realize that it was either take
the leg or take nothing, and he gave up and tried it on. The leg
is heavy, being hand carved from a single piece of wood, but not
impossibly so, and if Bhagat will learn to walk on it, and keep
practicing, I think he will be able to use it for years to come.

The plight of any amputee in this country is desperate. There
is so much unemployment, and such keen competition for

jobs that a person who is handicapped in any way simply does not stand a chance. As a result many amputees are forced to become beggars. Some develop an amazing agility even without the aid of artificial limbs. I saw one beggar on the road a few weeks ago who so much interested me that I stopped the car to watch him. I wish I had been able to take a motion picture of him to show some of our handicapped patients at the hospital. He was a double amputee. One leg was gone, nearly to the hip, and his arm on the same side was also missing, except for a very short stump. Despite this handicap, which left his body so awkwardly off balance, he was loping down the road at a rapid pace. The only support for the whole right side of his body was a long stick tied to the stump of his arm. This he manipulated with practiced ease, swinging it back and forth in harmony with his stride, and managing not a clumsy hop, but an erect, smooth gait. This may not sound difficult, but anyone who is handicapped himself, or has ever worked with such cases, can imagine the determination and practice necessary to develop such balance and coordination. What a shame that someone with so much will power should be forced to beg for a living.

Ram and I are in the middle of another feud. This time the subject under dispute is his method of killing chickens. I suppose he has been using the same method ever since we arrived, but it has been my good fortune to be out of the house when the slaughter took place, so I remained unaware of his technique of execution. We buy all our chickens alive from a peddler who comes to the door carrying them in a flat basket, then they are kept, still alive, under a wash bucket in the back kitchen, until needed. I came home in the middle of the morning the other day, and as I entered the house the most hellish squawking broke out. It sounded as though at least twenty chickens were being plucked alive. I stuck my head through the kitchen door, and there was Ram, kneeling on the floor in front of a bucket of water, grasping a chicken in each hand. He was attempting to drown them by holding their heads under water. To make matters worse, they were continually struggling to escape, and each time a head came up, the poor hen would give an eerie screech and gasp horribly. And there was Nathan watching with the detached interest of the very young. I was absolutely transfixed. "Ram, for heaven's sake put down those poor chickens. What in the world are you doing?" I screamed —I had to scream in order to be heard. Ram dropped the chickens in surprise, and they skittered around the kitchen, bumping into each other and us, still squawking. "I fix you chicken for dinner, Mem-sahib," Ram explained patiently. "But Ram, you are hurting them." "Yes, Mem-sahib," he agreed, obviously puzzled by my reasoning. After all how could he cook chicken for dinner without hurting the chicken? "Ram, can't you just wring their necks?" I asked. "How you do that?" he inquired. "Well you just hold the chicken and twist his head. I think." "I never do that, Mem-sahib, you show me." Well, Mem-sahib had never done it either, and had no desire to begin. I craftily turned the subject to hatchets. "You hold his body, and Jugetram cuts his head off," I explained. "Maybe Jugetram cuts me," said Ram. "Well, you chop with the hatchet, and let Jugetram hold the chicken," I suggested. Jugetram started to inch his way to the door, revealing a certain lack of confidence in Ram's ability with a hatchet. "Mem-sahib, I hold chicken in water. That is best way," and Ram grabbed one of the chickens again. "No, no, absolutely not. I will not have it, Ram. Let the chickens go outside with the baby." I felt that the poor hens had earned a reprieve. It seemed to me that they were in the same position as the man being hanged when the noose broke. Tradition has it that he may not be hanged twice, and I am all for upholding tradition. At this writing the chickens are still scratching around outside, tied to the fence by a string on each leg. I told Ram, "No more chicken dinners," at least until we can arrange a more painless death. He is getting his revenge. Every night the goat meat gets tougher and tougher while he mutters to Bart about my ridiculous fondness for chickens. Bart, of course, is no help at all. He has never killed a chicken either, and my pleas for his assistance in a painless execution received the hypocritical reply: "The kitchen is your business, dear!"

Once a year all our houses are given an inside coat of white-wash. The painters started working in our compound about a month ago, and I eagerly awaited their arrival. Unfortunately, soon after they began work on a house down the street there was quite a scandal about a stolen wrist watch, and the whole group was thrown in jail. There matters stood until yesterday, when Ram woke me in the morning with the news that the painters had arrived. I assume that the matter of the watch has been cleared up to everyone's satisfaction, and certainly the painters do not seem to have been overly troubled by their stay behind bars.

Ram rushed me out of bed with the information that I must speak to the painters, and dashed off to fling my breakfast on the table. All the servants were engaged in a novel orgy of activity. Even the gardener had been drafted and was happily moving the chairs around with no discernible purpose in mind. Outside on the lawn were the painters, squatting beside their ladders, buckets and brushes, and evidently unmoved by the furious energy around them. My eggs were hard, cold, and resting in a puddle of grease. To retaliate I told Ram to give the painters cups of hot tea, and rubbed in my little victory by requesting that it be served nicely in cups and saucers on a tray, not in an old pan with a dipper. Then I took my coffee and joined the painters on the grass.

Ram glared at me through the window and mumbled under his breath what I imagined to be comments on mem-sahib's appalling lack of dignity and decorum. The eight ex-convicts and I enjoyed a friendly conversation hampered only slightly by a complete lack of English on their side, and an equal ignorance of Punjabi on mine. Ram marched out with the tea tray, his face frozen into lines of rigid disapproval. He served each of the men while at the same time pointedly ignoring them and gazing coldly into the far distance. What a snob he is! I could not resist inviting him to join us, but this barb he refused to dignify with a reply. The painters slurped their tea politely while I drank some more coffee and passed around cigarettes. Ram remained standing, arms folded, unavoidably a member of our little group. What the painters thought of this morning tea party I cannot even imagine. The tremendous natural poise and genuine courtesy common to almost all Indians enabled them to appear as relaxed as though sitting on the grass with me, drinking tea out of china cups, served, reluctantly, by a white-jacketed cook was an everyday occurrence. After this pleasing interlude, it was time to get down to business. This turned into a highly diverting four-way conversation. Ram explained to me just what he wanted the painters to do, then I repeated his instructions in a firm voice, while the men looked politely blank. Ram translated my words with emphasis and grim gestures, and listened to their reply. The reply was duly translated into English, Ram told me what to answer, I answered in English, and again Ram turned it back into Punjabi. I inquired, "Ram, why don't you just tell them what you want, yourself?" But this it seems cannot be done; the authority of a genuine mem-sahib is essential. Finally, after a good deal of frenzied haggling, and just as I thought they were all going to pick up their paint-brushes and go, a compromise was reached. They would give the kitchen and bathrooms two coats in return for not painting one bedroom. At my insistence they graciously agreed to include the servants' quarters in the general agreement, and the work began.

The paint here is a kind of whitewash about the consistency of skimmed milk. This the painters color with various powders, usually tan or blue. After the paint dries, it comes off if you touch it or rub against it, and of course it cannot be washed, so once a year is none too often to paint the walls in a house containing three children. The paint is applied with brushes which look like bunches of twigs tied together at one end. The painters dip these twigs into the paint buckets, and slap them against the walls, spattering whitewash in every direction. Before the actual painting can begin, every bit of movable furniture is carried from the house to the yard. This action was nearly completed; all the servants staggered in and out laden with tables, chairs and bric-a-brac. This was stacked in a neat pile near the house, and the gardener, assuming a ferocious glare, squatted by it to make sure that no one was tempted to remove anything. Inside the house the painters set up their ladders and six of them started bombarding the walls with paint, while two more crawled about the floor with rags, lethargically wiping up the excess, and themselves being showered with splashes from above. Ram and Jugetram hovered over the men, darting suspicious glances this way and that. Evidently the episode of the missing watch is not to be repeated here.

Lest anyone think that this was the end, that the painters whitewashed the required rooms in the given time, then packed up their paraphernalia and left, let me say not so. The painting continued for about two hours, but in this time there were four fifteen-minute smoking breaks during which the painters climbed down from their ladders, wiped off their hands and lit up for a friendly chat with each other. At the end of two hours, when one room was partially painted, an excited little man was seen sprinting up the driveway. He stopped outside our window and shouted in Punjabi. The painters promptly packed up brushes and ladders and proceeded to leave with their buckets. Ram shrugged, Jugetram shrugged, and I followed them out, inquiring feebly, "What is wrong?" The excited little man in the yard glared at me through enormous spectacles, and informed me that the painters were working on the wrong house, a mistake had been made, it was not our turn. He seemed to feel that this alarming state of affairs was entirely my fault, and I was so amused by righteous indignation that I did not argue the matter.

The painters left, all the furniture was moved back into the house, Ram snooped around for hours looking into cupboards and counting towels, and the living room remains a nonobjective creation of tan and white.

eleven

We have had a hectic few days. Tony managed to break his leg. It would be Tony. He must be one of these accident-prone individuals, and even though he always manages to survive somehow, I am not sure that I will indefinitely. He did not fall out of the mango tree, or off the roof, as I have been expecting momentarily ever since we arrived. He was merely indulging in some horseplay with a young boy who works as a servant for another family nearby. According to Tony, he was teaching this youngster a few of the elements of judo, but the Indian boy was too apt a pupil, and in swinging Tony around, let go when he should have hung on. I felt almost as sorry for the Indian boy as I did for Tony. He was completely crushed, and practically in a state of shock when he carried Tony in. He insisted on coming with us to the hospital, and turned pale when we learned that the leg was actually broken.

It was a pretty dismal few hours for everyone. I clucked around like a mother hen. First I comforted Tony with the news that he was the only American child here ever to break a leg, and would shortly be the proud possessor of a plaster cast which all of his friends could decorate with their names. Then I reassured the Indian lad that we did not feel him at all to blame, and were in fact grateful for his good sense in carrying

Tony all the way home. Bart arrived from the dam, pale and shaken. Dr. Babbar was a tower of strength, handling the X-rays and treatment despite the two of us. He even came to the house and sat by Tony's bed for several hours that night when Tony was restless and in pain.

It was a simple fracture of the lower end of the tibia, not serious, but just about the worst place to break a leg, since that part of the bone has an insufficient blood supply and takes ages to heal. The strain is over now for everyone. Tony has discovered that his cast is just the thing to crack nuts with, and is only slightly hampered by it, skidding around the floor on his rear end totally unmoved by any concern for the seat of his pants.

On Sunday we decided to get out of Nangal for the first time and enjoy a change of scene. We had a family discussion about which direction to take, settled, as usual, by Ram, who voted for Chandigarh. The choice was eagerly seconded by Jugetram, who has a brother there. Any objections we might have felt about making such a trip in order to enable the servants to hold a family reunion were unspoken since they had both left to change into their best clothes. Chandigarh is the new capital of the Punjab. The old capital, Lahore, ended up on the Pakistan side after partition. This new capital is a proud Indian accomplishment. The government imported the famous architect Le Corbusier to design the major buildings and direct the planning of the entire city. It is to be most modern indeed, and though not yet completed is already the site of many government departments. Because this government is socialistic, it is involved in many more industries and activities than our government might be, and hence Chandigarh is as complex as one of our larger state capitals.

The servants packed a picnic lunch for us and, jammed into the car, we started our sixty-five-mile jaunt. At home a trip of sixty-five miles is nothing. People in California drive that far to see a movie or to watch a ball game, but in India the distance is really too far to attempt in one day. The road, which is a good one by Indian standards, is a narrow two-lane affair. Crowded on these two lanes are bullock carts, camel caravans, herds of cattle and goats, bicycles, pedestrians, huge top-heavy buses, religious processions, donkey trains, marriage parties, chickens, pigs, and dogs, all of them proceeding up the center of the road, and all of them utterly oblivious to motor traffic. Because automobiles are so infrequent, it is dangerous to drive closely behind another car. People will make way for the first car, only to move back blindly into your path. No doubt they feel that the car for the day has passed when the man in front of you goes by. We were never able to go more than thirty miles per hour, and many times were at a complete standstill, waiting for bullock carts to decide which way to move. When you travel here you must keep one hand almost constantly on the horn. Polite little honks mean nothing, for nobody takes them the least bit seriously. One must blast and blast before people decide that you really wish to get by, and move leisurely to the side of the road.

Even a short trip in India contains an element of adventure totally lacking in America. You never know when your road will come to an abrupt halt at the bank of some creek or stream and nonchalantly begin again on the other side. We jolted enthusiastically through a number of these brooks, but paused to consider when the road ceased to exist at the edge of a broad river bank. Far away across the river we could see our road unwind again into the distance. Its very existence seemed to prove that the river could be crossed. In front of us lay several miles of sand, rocks and gravel, in the center of which lay the actual river channel, wide and water-filled. Ram and Jugetram were undismayed by the prospect before us, but since they are also of the opinion that automobiles can climb trees, we were not impressed with their optimism. Finally we decided to drive down nearer the water, eat our lunch and await developments. Soon developments arrived in the shape of a large bus. Indian buses appear to have very narrow wheel bases and this one was filled with people hanging half in and half out of the windows, while on the roof was a shifting pile of bicycles, bed rolls and luggage. Swaying madly from side to side, it bumped across the sand toward us, looking very much like a stout man on roller skates. Without a second's hesitation, it careened into the water, churning up a small tidal wave on either side, and, diving crazily from pothole to pothole, finally emerged triumphant on the other bank. Once there it shuddered to a watery halt while the passengers crawled from it to give us shouts of encouragement and cheer. Ram said the bus would pull us out, if we got stuck. Bart set his face in stern lines of determination, reminiscent of our forefathers crossing the Plains, and we started in. It was tremendously exciting to pass through with the water rising about us and a complete lack of confidence in whether or not the river bottom would be there from one moment to the next. It usually was not, but we managed to avoid the truly bottomless holes, finally lurching up beside the bus. We indulged in a round of mutual congratulations with the driver and all the passengers, then piled back into our separate vehicles. Waving and shouting goodbye, everyone much refreshed by our little baptism, we drove on.

The site chosen for the building of Chandigarh has been the subject of much controversy. It is being erected on the hot, dry, dusty plains within just a few miles of much cooler and more beautiful mountain spots. Mainly because there has been no attempt at landscaping as yet, the setting appears drab. So far it is only a cluster of buildings set in the midst of barren fields. We drove directly to the apartment where Jugetram's brother lived, and he at once offered to conduct us on a guided tour of the city. We drove through the bazaar, which was more compact and somewhat cleaner than most, and through many broad streets lined with utilitarian multiple dwellings or homes of spacious simplicity. My principal objection to the town was a certain lack of variety. All the houses of one style lined one street, while all those of another lined a second, and so on. Perhaps when they have been individually landscaped the monotony will not be so evident, or perhaps the effect is intended to be one of ordered regularity, and only my point of view is at fault. Most of the houses and apartments are occupied by state employees, judges, lawyers, clerks, and servants. Since housing is generally furnished to government workers here, all those who earn a certain salary are housed in their particular category of dwelling. This rigid adherence to a social segregation based on income and position is somehow distasteful to me, but we follow the same custom on our Army posts, so I suppose that again it is my viewpoint.

Although many of the larger buildings have not yet been completed, the High Court Building is finished. It is one of the most compelling examples of modern design I have ever seen. Bart disliked its many unusual features and his objections may be well taken, although I am afraid part of his bias stems from a traditional lack of sympathy between architect and engineer. He felt strongly that it must have been expensive to build, but I am not convinced that unusual design is necessarily expensive design. The entire building is open and air-swept, with ramps and angles hard to describe. It does not look like India, but neither does it ape ancient Greece like so many of our own court buildings. It was a strange experience to see a building so new in conception set in the midst of a culture so old. The contrast was made even more sharp when a snake charmer with his pipe and cobras began his ritual on the steps. How hard it is for India to leap from the very old to the very new, when she has been forced by necessity to leap over all the stages between.

After our tour of the city we dropped the servants off for a visit with their families, and parked the car near where some children were playing cricket. From their enthusiasm we might have been watching sand-lot baseball at home, and although we did not understand the game, it was exciting. Many of the boys and frequently young men passing by stopped at the car to speak to us. This completely unself-conscious curiosity is irritating to some Americans but I am curious myself, and these informal conversations are frequently interesting. Invariably the Indian participant is courteous, often offering to bring tea or cold water. Just as we were beginning to worry about getting back across the river before dark, the servants appeared and we started the return trip. We reached the river while there was still a little light in the sky, and plunged into the water like veteran travelers. The dark road was nearly free of its assorted daytime traffic, and for miles the only signs of life we saw were the eyes of jackals gleaming at us from the roadside. As we neared Nangal we met a camel caravan plodding methodically along. Each camel had a bell hung around its neck which rang softly at every step sending out a lovely medley of sound.

The spring here has been very short, and it is almost hot again. I have enjoyed the brisk winter, but for the sake of the people, I am glad it is over. The villagers suffer when the weather is cold and frequently the temperature has been down to the freezing mark. The houses in this part of the country are ill suited to cold, the people have little warm clothing, and fuel is very scarce. All winter long I have watched children playing in our yard, wearing nothing but thin cotton shifts, their lips and toes blue with cold, their teeth chattering as they hugged themselves and hopped up and down in a vain effort to keep warm. I passed out so many of the boys' warm sweaters, shirts and jackets that they ended the winter with nothing left and we have had to have more made. Frequently I have dressed a seven- or eight-year-old warmly only to have her appear in a few hours, again stripped, the clothing preempted for younger brothers and sisters. The girls seem to get the worst of it, but to the credit of these loving children, I doubt that they even mind. Most of them are so sincerely devoted to the babies of their family that it is difficult to make them keep anything for them-

selves. So often I have distributed fruit or candy among a group
of children, only to have the older little girls thank me politely
and promptly hand their share to the younger ones. For a
hungry child to give up the chance for any kind of food is an
act of unselfishness of which few of our children would be
capable.

This is a barren land, far different from the tropical forests
farther south, which many people consider typical of India.
Trees of any kind are not common here. There are mango
orchards, and usually several sturdy old trees in each village, but
compared to our American suburbs where every house is surrounded by a variety of fruit and shade trees, there are few
indeed. Most of the trees line the roads, and these have been
deliberately planted and nursed to maturity. They are considered valuable, so that each is carefully numbered, and the
district engineer in charge of the section of road is also responsible for each tree, and must account for any damage befalling
it. It is impossible simply to plant a tree as we do at home. The
wandering cattle and hungry goats would strip it of foliage and
devour it before it had a chance to grow. Instead each tiny tree
must be fenced in with a tubular tower of thorns and brambles
which is made higher as the tree grows. Only after the maturing
branches are high enough to be out of reach of the marauding
animals is the tree safe. Consequently wood is scarce, expensive,
and seldom used for fuel by the people. We burn it, along with
a type of soft coal, which is also too costly for the villagers. The
most common fuel here is dried manure. Many Americans find
this strange, forgetting that our Plains people burned buffalo
chips a hundred years ago. Gathering up the manure is a continuous year-round job. Once gathered it is piled in the courtyard of each hut. When enough has accumulated the women
and children mix it with straw, twigs and even dirt, then mold
it into small flat cakes. These cakes are plastered to the sides
of the dwelling to dry, and when dry added to one of the cone-
shaped piles which form the village fuel supply. When burned

it provides an inefficient heat with little real warmth. The use of manure for this purpose, after all, is a matter of necessity, not of choice, but it is a practice which is devastating to the land which so badly needs the natural nourishment of fertilizer.

The winter weather creates problems at the hospital also. When it turns cold, the patients who fill the halls and open verandas during the summer are moved into a large unheated shed. In fact, all but three rooms of the hospital are unheated. We have a forced air heater which keeps two wards and the operating theater at a bearable temperature. The heated wards we fill with the most critical patients and postoperative cases. Even the labor room is unheated, and the women deliver their babies in a night temperature of forty degrees. We have one heavy wool blanket for each patient, and since there is no surplus, these grow more and more soiled as the winter wears on and the patients come and go. During the day, all the patients who are able drag themselves out into the sunshine to lie on the ground and soak up a little warmth. The malnutrition of the people makes the cold harder for them to bear. As I have mentioned before, we have barrels of dried milk given us by the Red Cross. Unfortunately it is supposed to be given only to children and pregnant and nursing mothers. Also we are required to keep careful records of who receive it, their age, weight gain, and so forth. These rules would doubtless be sensible under different circumstances, but under our conditions it is almost impossible to comply. We are too understaffed to have time for accurate records, and we have a very small proportion of pregnant or nursing mothers among our patients since most women here are still delivered at home. As Dr. Babbar says, "How can you justify giving milk to a sick child, but withholding it from a man whose several children will starve until we can cure him?" On the theory that it is vitally important to heal men who are often the sole support of their families as quickly as possible, Dr. Babbar gave orders some time ago that each patient in the hospital, regardless of age or sex, receive one cup of milk per day. When it became increasingly cold, we walked through the wards at night to the sound of hollow coughs and chattering teeth, and he ordered a second cup of milk to be given hot at bedtime to each patient. Sometimes we are given a sack of sugar, and we stir a little into each cup to give them a tiny bit of the energy they all so desperately need. How we will be able to square this with the Red Cross, I don't know. I only hope we will be able to get more milk when our present supplies have been exhausted.

The cold weather brings a change in the types of disease we are called upon to treat. Malaria and typhoid cease to be our killers, and to take their place we have pneumonia, diphtheria and mastoid infections. On the whole we have fewer patients, but we perform a greater percentage of operations. All eye surgery, tonsillectomies, and operations for chronic disorders are pushed through as rapidly as possible while the temperature is down. Of course we must perform emergency surgery continually during the summer months, but bacteria thrive on warmth, we must fight dust and flies; and perspiration and secondary infections make the healing of incisions more difficult when it is warm. So we finish all that we can while the weather keeps these difficulties at a minimum.

But as I said, the winter is over now. I have made a vow not to complain of the heat no matter how unpleasant it becomes this year, since I have seen what the cold means to people here. But I suppose when my clothes start sticking to me and my bed is clammy five minutes after I lie down, I will gripe just like everyone else.

twelve

I have been ill for nearly a month with malaria and its after-effects. It is an insidious disease, for you burn with fever, then shake with chills, and when it is over you are completely without energy. I am still taking quinine, which makes my head ring like an electric guitar. It is almost impossible to avoid contracting malaria here. We use mosquito nets at night and spray the house with DDT, but still those little nibbling bugs are abroad in the evening and early morning, and the chance of eventually being bitten is very good. There are several different strains of malaria, and here we have them all. Taking the modern malaria preventatives, such as atabrine, is unwise for a number of reasons. Usually these kill only one or two of the malaria strains and merely suppress the others. Consequently you may never suffer from a typical malarial attack, but the parasite is in your blood stream, weakening you and ready to strike when your resistance is low. Then too, all malaria preventatives must be taken with methodical regularity in order to be effective. Few people can be relied upon never to miss a single dose. Most of us would simply take one when we happened to think about it, and when we have forgotten, take two to make amends. This haphazard dosing invites a nice chronic case of low-grade malaria with such confusing symptoms that the poor doctor will not know whether to treat you for undulent fever or typhoid. Here in the hospital we still use clumsy old-fashioned quinine, because, as with the preventatives, most of the newer cures are only completely effective against a few of the malarial strains. Needless to say, we do not have the laboratory facilities for diagnosing the particular parasite involved, and in fact with our only equipment—a microscope—we are often unable to detect whether or not we have a case.

As Dr. Babbar says, "If I waited to get a positive malaria slide before I gave quinine, half the patients here would die." Malaria is a killer. It is a killer even though we know precisely what causes it and exactly how to cure it. It kills with its speed, and it kills by its ability to remain dormant within the blood stream until a time when its victim has been brought low by some other disease and it can strike with impunity. Malaria haunts the hospital, peering out from behind the mask of every ailment we treat. We perform an operation on an apparently healthy man, and the next day the quiet parasite he harbored within strikes, and he is shaking with fever. We see accident cases brought in, and even as we are treating their injuries, we must hurriedly rush for quinine. Most Indians of the poorer class by the time they reach maturity have chronic low-grade malaria. They are constantly weakened by low fevers, their spleens grow large, and they have little strength, but they have built up a resistance which enables them to avoid acute attacks as long as they remain otherwise healthy. The children are less fortunate. Many babies die for each one that manages to resist and live. In children, malaria is fantastically rapid in its ability to destroy. The other day at the hospital I took the temperature of a three-year-old who had just been brought in for treatment. The mercury rose above one hundred and seven degrees, and a few minutes later she died in my arms, before the quinine injection could work. She had been ill only a few hours, and had been brought to us as soon as possible from a nearby village.

Any suspicion I might have entertained that my affection for the servants was one-sided has certainly been dispelled by my illness. Ram has hovered over me like a flustered rooster, appearing constantly with cold limeade or chicken broth. Several times when the fever was worst I would waken to find his hand on my forehead, and drift back to sleep with his fierce Indian equivalent of "tut-tut" in my ears. Jugetram has tiptoed around with a doleful face, coming in my room twenty times a day to inquire in a voice of intense gloom, "O.K., Mem-sahib?"

During these days I have thought much about the conversation I had with an American friend regarding a two-day visit she paid to an English acquaintance in New Delhi. This Englishwoman had had the same cook for fifteen years and the same bearer for over ten. Yet she had made it a point never to learn their names. She had not the remotest idea whether they had children, or even how they lived. In fact she claimed never to have conducted any conversation with them that was not directly concerned with the management of her home. What a fantastic lack of ordinary human curiosity! I have no idea whether this woman's attitude toward her servants can be considered typical of the English in general, but *she* felt it was, and said so. According to her, Americans simply do not know how to treat their servants. They say please and thank you, they request instead of order, and, worst of all, they insist on treating their servants as human beings. "It is a great mistake to treat any of these people as though they were equals," she said. "They are not civilized, and it will be many years before they become so."

According to my friend, this woman's servants were much better trained than ours, neater, more polite, and quick to obey her least command. However, I am sure they never scold her for drinking too much coffee, refuse to wake her in the morning because she has been "working too hard," hide her money in a safe place when she leaves it forgetfully all over the house, or join her in an evening cigarette to discuss the events of the day. I am sure her servants' children do not call her mommie, or run across the yard to catapult into her arms when they see her coming, or play ring-around-a-rosy with her, or bring her little gifts of flowers and bright ribbons when she is ill. Nor, I imagine, would her servants' wives ever feel free to ask her to watch their children while they run an errand, or permit her to bake an Indian pancake on their charcoal oven, and shout with laughter if she burns it, or when she is ill come silently several times a day to sponge her forehead and rub her back. Nor would she probably consider any of these things either desirable or dignified. It depends, I suppose, on whether or not you wish to be served by well trained, impersonal automatons, or in an atmosphere of informal affection and mutual respect.

However, in all fairness I must admit that she is quite right in her statement that "Americans do not know how to handle servants." None of us here has ever had a servant; few Americans do. My closest contact with the American equivalent was a part-time cleaning girl employed by my mother-in-law. She not only drove a more expensive car than either of us, but was as well educated. It would hardly have occurred to her, or to us, that she was anything other than an equal. So, Americans are ill prepared to direct a houseful of servants, and how successfully they do so depends on their ability to adjust to the situation and on the personalities of the servants they employ. Many Americans expect impossible standards of service, corresponding to impeccable butlers and cowed parlor maids in English novels. When their servants fail to live up to these expectations, the American feels somehow cheated, and blames them for masquerading under false pretenses. Some Americans attempt to ape British and Indian methods and treat their servants with formality and rigid discipline. To the English, and to most wealthy Indians, this behavior is probably quite natural and matter of fact. To an American, it is not. In assuming it, they are assuming a pose and attempting to counterfeit a type of behavior quite foreign to them. That this pose is completely artificial soon becomes obvious to their servants. On the other hand, to treat your servants with complete informality as I do, is not always successful either. Many of them are so totally unused to this type of treatment that they become bewildered and confused. Or they may interpret your friendliness as a lack of assurance, as many times it may be, and proceed to take every advantage of it. There seems to be no easy solution for Americans inexperienced with this problem, but I would propose two axioms. First, never keep in your employ any servant whom you find yourself unable to like, or at least respect; and second, treat your servants in a way that is completely natural to you, relying on them to sense the honesty of your behavior, whatever it may be.

The grave danger of the false assumption that because two people both speak English they necessarily understand each other was brought home to me graphically the other day. One of the Indian nurses from the hospital came to me in tears. She was completely shaken and confused by an argument she had just had with an American woman. It seems that a few days before she had purchased an ironing board from a family returning to the States, and the American had offered to keep it for her until she could arrange to transport it to her quarters. The nurse had made the arrangements and sent a boy with a note to fetch the board. Much to her dismay the American lady had then descended on her waving the note and obviously intensely angry. The little nurse asked me to tell her what she had done wrong. The misunderstanding became obvious when I read the note. "My dear Mrs. Jones," it said. "Please hand over my ironing board." I tried to explain that the phrase "hand over" might, by an American, be considered rude, since to us it implies an unwillingness to give up the object in question. The girl agreed that my American neighbor had so interpreted the note, and indeed had hotly denied any intention of trying to "steal" the board. "But I never said she was trying to keep my board," the nurse told me. "I only asked her to give it to me now." No doubt that was her intention, but what she wrote was "hand it over." My explanation did not improve matters very much since the nurse resented any inference that she did not write correct English. "I have written English all my life. It is more my native tongue than Hindi. No one has ever before said I was rude," she informed me indignantly.

The fact that we both use English as a common language has blinded most Indians and Americans alike to the fact that it frequently hinders rather than helps our understanding of each other. Between the British-English spoken by educated Indians and the colloquial American-English we speak, there is an ocean of difference. Identical words carry quite separate meanings, and what may be perfectly polite to them, to us is rude in the extreme. On the other hand we must constantly impress them in the same way. Yet we are each convinced we are speaking the language of the other.

One fundamental area of misunderstanding, which would be funny if it were not so troublemaking, is the American's reliance on swearwords to amplify his vocabulary. Evidently the British swore very little, or only when intensely angry, so that the Indians are completely nonplussed by the American custom of scattering invective in every direction, under every circumstance. When an American comes up behind an Indian, hits him on the back, and says, "Well you blankety-blank old blank!" the Indian may perhaps be forgiven if he does not immediately appreciate the fact that he is being greeted as an old friend. Since American construction men possess a large and colorful vocabulary, of the sort employed by Marine sergeants, their orders and directions on the job are usually well larded with fine old Anglo-Saxon. Completely mystified, the Indians never know whether they are receiving a deep personal insult or being complimented on a job well done.

Luckily few Indian workmen understand enough English, Anglo-Saxon or otherwise, to know when they are being sworn at, and their most frequent reaction is to nod, smile happily and say, "Thank you, Sahib!" And many of the younger Indian engineers are adopting our more pithy phrases with the cheerful innocence of schoolboys.

Nathan is speaking Punjabi. The servants have been claiming for months that he was learning their language, but we felt their imagination was working overtime. To us he sounded the same as he has for a year, gabbling his own language, and apparently surprised when no one understands him. But my days in bed have persuaded me that the servants are right. While his only English remains "mommie" and "daddy," I have heard him outside my window chattering in Punjabi with Jugetram's two children. My recent attempts to converse with him in either language have been most unsatisfactory. When I speak English, he looks at me blankly and turns to Ram for a translation. When I try out my limited Punjabi, he also turns to Ram, to complain, also in Punjabi, "Mommie does not talk very well, does she?" The servants think that this is a most amusing situation, and I am sure will encourage him to speak only their tongue. He spends every waking moment with Caca and Bimela, Jugetram's boy and girl, and has very little interest in any of the American children of his own age. In fact he claims to be "Punjabi" and all his actions are more Indian than American. Certainly he is a walking monument to the effects of environment. He crouches on his heels in the Indian way; he does not like our food, but devours chapatty and curry; and he likes to sleep curled up in a heap with Bimela and Caca. The three of them look like a tousle-headed litter of warm kittens, one blond and two dark. The only thing that I insist upon is that he practice American toilet habits, since following the Indian custom in this respect would certainly get him into trouble at home. Except for the talking, which is a recent accomplishment, his Indianizing has been a slow process over the months we have been here.

Needless to say, many of the Americans are highly disapproving. I well realize that he is going to be forced into major readjustments when we leave here, but I hope that he will be old enough by then to understand something of their necessity. In the meantime, the only way I could reverse the process and Americanize him would be to discharge the servants and remove him entirely from Indian influence. Since he loves them all with the utter dependence of a two-year-old, this course would seem cruel in the extreme. Besides, Nate is a completely lovable, happy, normal baby, and I cannot feel that he has been anything but benefited by his exposure to Indian methods of child rearing.

For lack of reading material I have been forced to give more careful attention to Indian newspapers, with a great deal of resulting amusement. Since much of the Indian press seems to be, if not communist, certainly not prowestern, there is a great deal in it to antagonize any American. The small local papers, however, seem willing to leave the propaganda department to their big city brothers, and concentrate on reporting, matter-of-factly, neighborhood events which seem novel indeed to me. Most intriguing were two recent items.

This part of the Punjabi is the home of groups of highwaymen known as dacoits. These aggressive individuals hide in ambush along the roads to rob unwary travelers, and are not always adverse to a little murder, now and then. Needless to say the police frown on such activities and are continually setting up elaborate traps to snare one or another band. One newspaper item had to do with the failure of such a trap.

"Police, last night, hid in waiting to catch a band of dacoits operating in this area. Secret information led them to believe the thieves were planning an ambush. A large group of dacoits did appear, but something caused their suspicions to be aroused, and before the police could restrain them, they separated and fled in the darkness. In running away they were forced to leave behind a large elephant. Our police have arrested this elephant, which is obviously implicated in recent robberies, and have detained him in the prison compound."

The second item is self explanatory.

"Police report that late last night our police station was entered by a horde of large monkeys. These monkeys were very bold, tearing up files of papers, and attacking the policeman on duty, who called for help. Other policemen rushing to his aid were unable to chase off the animals, and it was decided to draw pistols in the hope that the gunshots would frighten them away. A number of shots were fired. The monkeys quickly ran. Unfortunately several of our policemen were found to have been wounded by bullets, and are now in the hospital."

A fascinating custom in regard to the Indian methods of treating criminal suspects has recently become known to me. Several times I have noticed Dr. Babbar giving thorough physical examinations to different men. I never paid much attention, assuming it was in connection with job fitness or accident compensation. The other day I was in his office when three rascally-looking Hindus entered. Without thinking he started to address them in English, and I heard, "What have you done?" before he lapsed into Hindi. Their answers seemed to amuse him, and he nodded to me and said, "Dacoits." I watched the examination, and saw that most of it consisted of a careful search for any sign of bruises on their skin, climaxed when all three sat in a row and elevated their legs so the doctor could see the soles of their feet. When the examination was over, Dr. Babbar filled out a lengthy report in duplicate, on each man, noting the exact size, shape and position of every scratch and bump on his body. Each man was handed one copy, and Dr. Babbar ordered the originals to be locked in his safe. When the men had left, I asked Dr. Babbar what it was all about. He seemed surprised by my ignorance, but explained the procedure to me.

It seems that these were, indeed, dacoits from a nearby village. They had reason to believe that someone had informed against them, and that the police would soon arrest them all.

American "third-degree" methods are not approved here, in theory, but in practice, as in our country, they are sometimes used. These men felt it was likely they might be beaten in an effort to make them name their accomplices. To forestall this, they had come for certificates of health from the Medical Officer of the district. "Now what will happen?" I asked. "Well," said the doctor, "they will have to turn themselves in at once. If they wait for the police to catch up with them, it might be several days. Then their certificates will not mean very much, since the police could claim that any further bruises had been received between the time I saw them and their arrest." "If they go to the police now they can't be beaten?" I inquired. "Oh, no," he answered. "If the police make any threats against them they will show my certificates. Then the police will know that I have the originals locked in my safe and can testify at any trial that any further marks had been caused by them." Dr. Babbar feels it is a practical way to assure that the police are not tempted to resort to violence, and expressed amazement that we had not developed a similar means of safeguarding our suspects from ill-treatment. I think the system is not only practical, but reveals a high regard for individual rights.

Something has happened which has finally brought from Ram a grudging approval of my work at the hospital. Always before he has been puzzled and unsympathetic with my nursing activities. At times when I have enlisted his help in cooking food for someone or translating for me, he has been openly hostile. Once when he came to the wards and found me on my hands and knees scrubbing a bed, he was so shocked that he turned around and left without speaking. But now one of *his* relatives is ill, and his attitude has undergone an abrupt change.

Ram calls this man his cousin, which probably means he is a more distant relative than that, since, if he were really a cousin, Ram would refer to him as a brother. At any rate his "cousin" was on his way to Nangal from a village nearby when he was bitten on the foot by a viper. I know nothing about poisonous snakebites, and this is the first case I have seen here. The country about has numerous types of deadly snakes including cobras, kraits and several kinds of vipers. The reason that we are not called upon to treat more cases must be because the venom works so terribly fast. Absolutely the only chance for survival for anyone bitten is an immediate injection of antivenom serum which is only available at the scattered hospitals and clinics. Many people must die before they have a chance to reach us. Indeed, the attack would have to take place very close by for anyone to get here in time. This man was just outside of town when the snake struck. His companions showed remarkable good sense by lifting him into a passing rickshaw and racing immediately to the hospital. The usual Indian habit is to hunt around for the snake to see if it is a venomous one; if it is the person bitten will by that time be dead.

The cousin was already unconscious by the time he arrived, although only a few minutes had passed. Dr. Babbar sent for me, knowing I would be interested. By the time I left the nearby ward where I had been working, the man had already been given an antivenom injection, and Dr. Babbar was excising and cleaning the area of the bite itself. I was still watching and helping when Ram arrived. He was as upset as I have ever seen him, and kept saying, "Mem-sahib, you fix him?"

I think the man will live. Large areas of capillary veins have ruptured beneath his skin, so that he looks as though he had received a horrible beating, but he has regained consciousness. There is a certain notoriety connected with surviving a snakebite, and Ram is basking in reflected fame. I told him that he must feed his cousin from our kitchen, and see that he has everything he needs. "Use your food, Mem-sahib?" he asked. "Of course, Ram, use our food, and make him lots of cool drinks." Ram looked puzzled again. "Mem-sahib, he is my cousin. Why you give him food? *I* give him food." I agreed, "Ram, he is your cousin, so you must feed him some of your food, but you need food too. You cannot buy limes. You do not have ice. I have these things which your cousin needs, so you must use them." I used an Indian way of making my position clear, which sounds affected when written down, but which Ram understood very well. I said, "Ram, you are my elder brother, so your cousin is also my cousin, and I must give him help." He looked at me intently for a minute or two, then said, "Mem-sahib-ji, you have many cousins at the hospital." Finally I have been able to make him understand why I work there.

The only outward sign of a change in our relationship is the fact that Ram now affixes -ji to the mem-sahib he has always called me. This little syllable literally means, "sir," but more informally is a symbol of either respect or affection, or both. He is also promoted and is now Ram-ji whenever I address him.

thirteen

I have started wearing saris lately. Many of my clothes have worn out in the hands of the dhobi. The poor little washerman was almost done in by seersucker. Evidently he considered it a challenge to his ability as an ironer, and every seersucker garment I brought over has had each pucker carefully ironed out. I cannot sew myself, and I cannot explain to the tailor here how to sew what I want, so saris seem to be the answer. I understand that, in the large cities of India, the wearing of saris is not considered "good form" among the smart European and American colonies. It seems one might be mistaken for a half-caste, or even an Indian, heaven forbid! Our women are quite willing, however, to adapt this charming garment to our own dress styles, thus tampering unnecessarily with something perfect as it is.

The Indians are delighted when a foreigner adopts their national dress, and I have been receiving continuous congratulations and advice from Indian women I scarcely know. The sari is really three separate garments: a long underslip which ties at the waist with a drawstring, a tight-fitting midriff-length blouse, and six yards of sari. The sari itself is tucked in around the drawstring of the underslip, then draped over the shoulder. Learning to drape this properly is not difficult, but keeping the material from slipping off the shoulder is a constant battle which even

the Indian women never entirely master. The secret of keeping
the sari safely anchored is to pull the drawstring very tight.
Many Indian women have a callus which runs clear around their
waists from this string, and how they can bear it so tight is a
mystery to me.

The sari is the national dress for all of India, but each region
has its own typical costume also, which is more often worn by
the common people. Here the garment worn by the village and
lower-class women is a kind of pajama suit. Upper-class ladies
also wear it for less formal occasions, and as a kind of housedress. The pajamas consist of pants which are very full around
the waist and narrow at the ankles, and a high-waisted blouse,
tight around the bust, then loose nearly to the knees. It is a very
awkward garment, unattractive on all but the most slender figures. The most charming dress of all is worn by the women
from the nearby mountain districts, and some of the gypsy road
workers. This is a tiny fitted bolero and an enormous, gathered
ankle-length skirt, both in very bright colors and usually decorated with quantities of bulky silver jewelry.

It seems strange that such a poor country would have developed so many types of dress, all of which are so extravagant
of materials and so clumsy and bulky to wear for active work.
The Chinese pajama suit seems admirably designed for simplicity and practicality by comparison. All the regional dresses of
this area, and of course the sari itself, take from six to eight
yards of material. Although cotton and silk are plentiful and
comparatively cheap, women who are very poor must make do
with one garment, when they could have two or three if the
styles were tailored from fewer yards of cloth. I cannot believe
that the sari would ever have continued very long as a popular
dress except in a country where servants are plentiful and inex-
pensive. Like our hoop skirts, they are exquisite to the observer,
but quite impossible for the wearer. As long as one can merely
be decorative it is all right, but the minute any kind of activity
is required you are hampered by yards of material flowing in

every direction. Even women who have worn saris for years are continually pulling, pushing and fooling with them to keep them out of their way. The pajama suit is much more practical except for the fact that a long narrow scarf, which also must be continually adjusted and rearranged, is always worn with it.

The most interesting thing about the sari is that it is as subject to continual style changes as our dresses. Without any help from Paris, fashion decrees changes year by year which are as radical to Indian women as the frequent raising and lowering of our skirts are to us. Most Indian ladies receive the bulk of their sari wardrobes at the time of their weddings, so a really fashion-conscious woman can tell almost exactly what year all of her friends were married merely by the style of their saris. None of the style changes is very obvious to an outsider. One year fashion will order wide bands of gold embroidery, the next year narrow bands of silver. Or heavy dark silk will lose its popularity to pastel chiffon. This year the most beautiful saris are delicately appliquéd with tiny sea shells and pearls, and many women are adopting plain saris of sheer nylon.

Young brides wear the darkest colors and the most jewelry. Generally a woman wears paler colors and less jewelry as she grows older, until after a certain age white is mostly worn. There are many exceptions, of course; just as in America a grandmother will occasionally wear a barebacked summer dress. The different saris are appropriate only for certain occasions. It is difficult for the uninitiated to know when she is wearing the correct sari, and I know I have several times been guilty of wearing a ball gown to a picnic and a housedress to a formal tea.

A most interesting case came into the hospital the other night. As far as I know this patient traveled the greatest distance to reach us of anyone for whom we have cared. About a year ago a man working at Bhakra developed acute appendicitis; we operated successfully, discharged him and thought no more about it. This man was from a village far across the mountains from us, only fifty miles or so from the border of Tibet. When he returned to his home and described his sickness and operation, he became a ten-day wonder. No one else in his village had ever had an operation, and to his people it was nearly a miracle that he had been opened up, without feeling pain, and lived. When months later another man in the same village developed a severe pain in his abdomen, our original patient was struck by the similarity of the symptoms, and intelligently concluded that this man probably also required an operation. Evidently it did not occur to anyone to seek a closer hospital. A man from their village had been cared for in Nangal and survived, so obviously that was the place to go. A group of the village men constructed a litter for their sick friend, and set off across the mountains carrying him. There are practically no roads in the district, so their forced march carried them up and down steep mountain trails, and across several streams. They finally arrived at the hospital, after having walked almost continously for nearly three days. It was late at night when they reached us. I was just leaving the hospital when I saw six or seven men set down a litter in front of our entrance, then collapse around it in apparent exhaustion. Even to a layman it was evident that the man on the litter was in desperate condition. Dr. Babbar was called and the man was put to bed. The doctor diagnosed not appendicitis, but an intestinal obstruction, a condition even more critical. The necessity for surgery was obvious, but the poor patient was so weak and dehydrated that we were forced to wait. We started giving him intravenous glucose, and shot him full of penicillin. Finally his condition improved slightly, and we knew his only hope was an operation during this brief improvement. We operated early in the morning, and although he is still on the critical list, there is every chance that he will survive. Everyone in the hospital seems to feel a personal responsibility for this case. We are so well aware of the courage shown by his friends in carrying him to us and their complete confidence in our ability to cure him was pathetic. It would have been heartbreaking to fail them.

We see many cases of intestinal obstruction here. This condition is just what its name implies. A section of intestine, for some reason, becomes obstructed or strangled, thus having its blood supply cut off and preventing the passage of the usual waste matter, which collects above the obstruction. If the obstruction is only a partial one there is less anxiety, but when there is a complete blockage, gangrene soon attacks the strangled portion, and peritonitis and death follow quickly. Although there can be a number of different causes, most of the obstructions we see are due to tuberculosis of the abdomen. In this disease, bands or adhesions may be formed in the abdomen, and occasionally a loop of intestine is pinched between them. When caught very early the operation is a simple one. The surgeon simply frees the trapped portion and allows it to resume its normal function. Still, as with most surgery cases, the patient usually delays until his condition is grave. I have been reading statistics in a British medical journal which give the mortality rate for this particular operation as nearly 80 per cent. I think it says a great deal for the quality of our surgery that even with inadequate facilities our mortality rate is only 40 per cent, and it can hardly be said that our patients are good surgical risks, or come to us early.

Dr. Babbar is a very daring surgeon. He never hesitates to perform an operation when death is the only immediate alternative. He has never lost a patient on the table, which is a miracle considering the condition of many on whom he operates. Frequently patients react to surgery in a way no book describes. Those who have almost no detectable pulse or blood pressure seem to rally under the knife quite contrary to all expectation. Any kind of surgery is bound to present a shock to the system, and anesthesia also presents a risk to someone already nearly dead. Why is it then that some patients who are barely alive react quite differently, and revive to a detectable extent while on the table? I wonder whether it is possible that when the body reaches a certain critical stage, the normal reactions are reversed?

A month or so ago a young bride was carried in almost completely paralyzed. She had tuberculosis of the spine, and the infected bone was pressing on the spinal cord. She had lain in this condition for weeks, and only the obvious fact that she was dying had finally moved her relatives to seek help. The girl was pathetically wasted, weak and semiconscious. We were barely able to detect a pulse and blood pressure. The anesthetist refused to participate in any operation which he felt would end quickly and fatally. Dr. Babbar discussed his point of view with me. "Carol," he said, "this girl will die. She is dying now. No drug or medicine can possibly help her in time. The only chance for her that exists is to remove the bone which is causing her paralysis, and clean out the worst of the infection. Then we can treat her tuberculosis and build up her strength. She may well die during the operation. If not, she may die following it from shock. But she is going to die soon anyway, and I do not feel it is right to deny her the only gamble she has."

He ordered the operation, and performed it under local anesthesia almost entirely, deadening the area with successive injections of novocaine as he worked. It was such a fantastic demonstration of skill that the other doctors are still discussing it, and the gamble was successful. The little bride has made steady improvement, and I am giving her physical therapy every day in the hope that she will eventually regain the use of her legs.

To those who still believe that life is cheap in the East, I can only say that it is not cheap to the people who live it, or to the Indian doctors who try to help them.

My curiosity about doings at the hospital led to an interesting encounter last Sunday. I was in the yard playing with the children when I noticed a strange car parked in front of the hospital, and, with my usual inquisitiveness, went over to see what was going on. I found two bewildered newspapermen in-

volved in a situation every American here dreads. They had
come, with their wives, to cover the dedication ceremony of a
powerhouse near here. As they had barely started their return
trip to New Delhi, an old man had veered over from the side of
the road and walked directly into the side of their car. Leaving
their wives standing by the road, they had lifted the old man
onto the back seat and started back to Nangal where they knew
there was a hospital. We introduced ourselves and I learned
that one was John Hlavacek, the American representative of
UP in India, and the other, Alex Campbell, was the correspondent for *Time* magazine. They were in an awful state of
mind, trying to find out how badly the old man was injured,
concerned about their wives standing alone in the hot sun, and
uncertain just what action they should take.

We got the patient settled and the duty doctor made a
superficial examination. Then I took Mr. Hlavacek and Mr.
Campbell to our house to wait for the police and decide what
should be done. Bart took our car and drove out to find Mrs.
Campbell and Mrs. Hlavacek. When they arrived back, hot and
tired, the police made their appearance. Despite the fact that
driving is such a hazard here, and the major part of the Indian
population is so careless in their behavior toward motor traffic,
a motorist who hits a pedestrian is assumed to be in the wrong
unless the facts prove otherwise. For an American accidentally
to injure an Indian is much, much worse than for an Indian to
do so. Often the police are prejudiced, and will do little or
nothing to discover the true facts of the case. Although in the
long run it would be difficult to jail an American, it is still
possible to involve him in endless difficulty with court appear-
ances, fines and so forth. Of course I do not mean to plead
that Americans should be allowed to drive recklessly, heedless
of the damage to anyone we hit. It is right that the responsibility for any accident be assessed, as would be done with any
accident occurring in America. But in our own country we are
familiar with the laws, we know that our police will have scien-

tific equipment to assess the value of our story, and quite often there will be testimony of unbiased witnesses to support us.

Fortunately for our new-found friends, a young English-speaking Indian had witnessed the accident. He was a workman at Bhakra, and unaffected by any sort of prejudice. His description of the accident was exactly the same as that given by the drivers of the car: the old man was walking down the side of the road; as the car approached, it slowed and the driver sounded his horn; the man continued walking until, as the car was passing him, he turned suddenly and walked right into it. The importance of his testimony was obvious, but it was soon equally obvious that the police preferred to disbelieve him. They thought, or wanted to think, that he had been bribed. You cannot imagine how uncomfortable it is to be involved with the police of another country. Much of the time they spoke to each other in Punjabi, leaving us completely in doubt about what was going on and what action would be taken. Although the man in charge was polite enough, I had always had the feeling that he disliked Americans intensely, and his very evident disbelief of everything we said seemed to confirm my opinion.

The police accompanied the two men to the scene of the accident, then returned to question everybody again. They went to the hospital, but the old man was still unconscious, although he seemed free of any injury, except a concussion. It was quite apparent that the two couples would not be permitted to leave for Delhi that night. "If ever" was an implication we ignored. Since there is a certain absence of first-class hotels in Nangal, we invited them to squeeze in with us. A lack of beds provided a problem, and I am afraid they did not spend a very comfortable night, especially since, in my delight at seeing some new faces, I kept everyone talking far too late. The next day the old man was declared conscious and out of danger. Dr. Babbar supported the story told by the journalists when he found the injured man to be totally blind and almost totally deaf. Poor old man. He did not even know he had been hit by a car, or where he was. Our attempts to explain what had happened were hopeless. He could not hear or see, and was too senile to understand. We were all much relieved that he seemed to be all right. The police relaxed their antagonism and, after taking names and addresses, gave permission to both couples to proceed on their way. I promised John Hlavacek to deliver the old man back to his village when he recovered and they each gave me some money to pay for any food and extra care he needed. I was much embarrassed by their thanks since I had enjoyed their company so much, and had even rather guiltily hoped that they might have to stay a little longer.

fourteen

We have kept our old man in the hospital longer than we would usually feel necessary, to make certain there would be no unforeseen aftereffects. But finally the police have given us permission to fulfill my promise and see him back to his village. He has been an unintentionally difficult patient. The whole time he has been with us he has never seemed able to understand where he was or why he was being kept in bed. Consequently, he would continually get up and wander off. The other patients were extremely good about trying to keep track of him, but I have been most concerned that he would manage to escape one night and wander blind and deaf through a strange town, frightened and alone. So I am much relieved to know that we can finally return him to his people, who, of course, have no idea of what has been happening to him all this time.

I used what was left of the money given me to buy him a new shirt and a really handsome turban. He was pleased as a child with his unexpected wardrobe, and wound and rewound the turban, pushing and patting it to just the right angle. I combed his beard, gathered his few possessions into a small parcel, and we were ready to go. That was when we ran into difficulties. I knew where the accident had taken place, and had intended to drive the car there and start making inquiries, but I decided first to get the patients to question the old man and see if I could at least learn the name of his village before starting out. They all lined up and yelled at him in shifts. He obligingly answered most of the questions, but when his answers were translated he appeared to have told each person a different story. He claimed residence in five or six different villages in widely different directions. Then the patients began to take sides and argue. One claimed to have seen him in a village some sixty miles from here, in a totally different area from where he had been hit. Other patients felt equally certain that they had seen him or heard of him in other villages far removed. The old man nodded happily at each name mentioned, while I became convinced that I would spend the next six months searching the whole Punjab for the place he called home.

It seemed sensible to start from the area where he had been found, and work back from there. Ram and I got him into the car, and we started out. He obviously did not remember his other trip in an automobile, and for the first few miles he was terrified. Finally Ram was able to make him understand that he was riding in a car; then he really began to enjoy himself, bouncing on the seat, and patting the dashboard. We pulled up at a tea stall not far from the accident site, and helped him out of the car. He startled us by immediately galloping off down the road heedless of danger. The amount of speed he managed was astounding. Ram and I had all we could do to catch up with him. We finally caught him, and each took his hand to forestall another foot race. Inquiries at the tea stall got us nowhere, but one of the men suggested that we go to the school nearby, in the hope that one of the children might be from his village. We left the road and guided our charge down the little trail to the school, followed by most of the tea stall customers. The school was being held under a huge mango tree. Fifty or sixty little boys sat cross-legged in a circle around the schoolmaster, busily writing on slates while he lectured. I picked my way through the children and explained to the teacher what our problem was. He graciously invited me to sit down, and I was afraid he would feel it necessary to send for refreshments. However, he contented himself with smiling at me, and described to all the children what had happened. He asked them to look carefully at the old man to see if they could recognize him. Like all little boys, the pupils welcomed the break with glee, and were obviously hopeful of prolonging it indefinitely. They surrounded the old man, peering at him with exaggerated intensity and chattering to each other in excited voices. I was more patient than the schoolmaster. He was quite unwilling to permit his school to indulge in such undisciplined behavior in front of a foreign stranger, and brought them back to attention with a few stern words.

When all was quiet once more he questioned the boys, and finally found two who remembered the old man. I felt somewhat doubtful of simply accepting the word of children, who might well be mistaken, so we led the two to the old man and tried to see if he knew them. But it was difficult to tell from his reactions whether he did or not. However, the boys insisted that the old fellow was well known in their village, since he frequently wandered off and was sometimes missing for days. They had found him twice and returned him to his people. One boy said that he did not know the old man for a few seconds because he was so much cleaner and better dressed than usual. I felt certain, after listening to their explanations, that they did indeed know him, and it was an immense relief to find his home so easily. I said goodbye to "baba," who at the last minute decided he did not want to leave my familiar voice, and the two schoolboys were excused from lessons to guide him home. I hope his family was glad to have him back, but I wonder if he was not a burden they would have been happy to be rid of.

Dr. Babbar and his wife had to go to the county seat, Hoshiapur, to appear in a court case, and they invited me to accompany them. Sheila Babbar is also a doctor, and a charming person, though more reserved than her husband. We started out in the doctor's small British car, and the first few miles were uneventful. We had only one river to cross, which at this time of the year should cause no difficulty. And indeed when we reached it, there seemed no reason to hesitate, so Dr. Babbar put the little car in low gear and we plunged in. This river, the Suwan, is several miles wide, with sand banks and gravel beds showing above the surface at the more shallow points. But even during this season of drought it can be treacherous, as we soon found, because its soft bed drags at the wheels of a car like quicksand.

We were only a short distance from our starting point when we hit a mire hole, drowned the motor, and came to a standstill. It was wonderful! Unfortunately my hosts did not share my enthusiasm for getting stuck in rivers, but they were able to glean a certain amusement from my obvious enjoyment. Mrs. Babbar was hampered by her long sari, but I had on a cotton dress, quite adequate for river wading so I slipped out of my shoes and squeezed out of the car. The water was almost hot, and the sandy bottom was perfect for squishing between the toes. Dr. Babbar issued a few dire warnings about the prevalence of hookworms in river sand, but finally he rolled up his pants legs and joined me. A truck full of workmen pulled up at the near bank and called and shouted to us. I waved back and continued splashing, but Dr. Babbar got his tow rope out of the trunk and tied it to the car's rear bumper. Several of the workmen waded in, and we all pushed from the front. The truck driver tied the other end of the tow rope to his bumper, and backed up his truck. Jolting and bucking the car finally arrived back at the river bank, where it stood dripping water from every pore. The workmen continued to be helpful, opening up the hood and blowing on various pieces of the motor. I waded around looking for bits of flint to take home to the boys. The blowing was apparently effective, for the engine finally started. I was wet to my waist, and the doctor was not in much better shape, but the sun was so hot we knew our clothes would dry immediately, and meanwhile their dampness was pleasantly cool. The truck driver offered to cross the river ahead of us, avoiding our hole, and giving us a path to follow. This time we navigated the several miles of churning water successfully and started up through the hills.

The country between Nangal and Hoshiapur, some sixty miles, is wild and primitive. The Americans call it leopard country, and the name fits. The hills are steep and rocky, cut through by deep gorges, and covered with scrubby trees and dusty foliage. It has the stern and uncompromising beauty that I love best. Here nature seems to say, "This is the way I am. You must like me either this way, or not at all. I will not lure you with blue lakes and flowers, with green grass and gentle pictures. Somewhere else I may please you by being merely pretty, but here I am real." The road was a terror. Narrow, blind curves made my heart stop as we careened around them, honking to announce our coming. Dr. Babbar drives skillfully, but seems to believe that every road is a speedway expressly designed for his driving. At the top of the mountains we stopped near a silent resthouse. These buildings, scattered about India in isolated areas, were used by the English officials as they traveled about the country conducting their business. Now most of them have been taken over by the Indian government which keeps them for the same purpose, but since roads have improved and traveling has become easier, they frequently remain empty for most of the year. This resthouse was built on a jutting cliff away from the road. We walked to it along a climbing trail, and the old caretaker greeted us happily. The wind tore roughly along the wide verandas, and we could see the whole valley spread below, cut by the curving river where we had waded an hour before. The caretaker told us the house was called Ban

Khandi, and that it had been there for years. The old house seemed to be clutching desperately at the barren rock, refusing to be shaken by the relentless wind. It made me think of the moors and crags of Wuthering Heights, and of all the other desolate houses that for hundreds of years have touched a particular lonely longing in men and women the world over.

We ate our picnic lunch on the porch with the monkeys chattering at us from the trees, and poking their faces daringly close in their search for crumbs. Then we got back to the car and drove on. In Hoshiapur we dropped Dr. Babbar at the courthouse and parked the car. Sheila Babbar had promised to show me the town, including the old bazaar. Hoshiapur is a very old city, almost untouched by anything remotely modern. Even the English bothered little with this country. It is inaccessible and poor, so there was no reason for them to be interested in it. We wandered through the narrow crooked streets to the place where an antiquated clock tower marked the beginning of the bazaar. For the first time I could see a real usefulness in the billowing folds of a sari. Sheila draped hers over her head and held it close to cover her nose and mouth. I had no such protection from the flies that hovered so thickly they were like a sticky black cloud. They flew in my mouth, crawled up my nose and lit on my eyelids until I thought I could not stand it. Everywhere I looked were flies; clustered in clumps on the children's running eyes, covering all the food displayed with a hovering black blanket, swarming in the open gutters with a frantic buzzing. Sheila laughed at me. "Well," she said, "you wanted to go through an old city. Here it is. You see there are no Americans here!" I was annoyed with myself for feeling such a western distaste for something that these people must live their lives with, so I forced myself to ignore the flies and the stench which was almost as nauseating, and see what I had come to see. I soon found, as always happens, that I became so engrossed in the color and noise and confusion that I forgot everything else. If you focus only on the dirt, the poverty, the sickness and the smells in India, you soon find yourself hating it all. But when you open your eyes and see that these hateful things are enmeshed in a busy tapestry which also contains the richness of life and the spirit of the people, they fade into a murky background against which the colors of laughter, vitality and courage are even more vivid.

I saw some sculpture around the entrances to many small temples, opulent figures of gods and goddesses all looking much too fertile to be worshiped discreetly. There were purdah balconies with peepholes, once the window on life below for proper Moslem ladies. I saw a public library, trim and proper, with clipped hedges and white paint, but not a single book lover to give it life. There were children everywhere, almost as thick as the flies, sucking on mangoes, petting the babies they carried astride their hips, chasing each other, laughing and playing among the stalls. Everywhere the heat and dust were heavy in the air, until the occasional shade of a giant mango with the light filtering down onto the bright clothes of the people resting beneath it seemed cool and quiet by comparison. I watched some wood carvers working on elaborate table designs, while the sweat streamed from their bodies. Sheila bought some cloth and I bought some simple handmade toys for the children. Then we walked back to meet the doctor.

I would have been lost forever in that bazaar without Sheila to guide me. We had twisted and turned along the narrow alleys until I was hopelessly confused, but she led the way with complete confidence, and soon we were back on the wider streets. I was just wondering if my Indian friends would find a trip through one of our large department stores as intriguing as I find their bazaars, when someone behind us yelled, "Hey!" Sheila walked on uncomprehending, but I turned to find an Indian at my heels, who promptly stretched out his hand. "You're an American, I bet!" he said. I admitted this was true, and I knew before he spoke again that he was also from my country. No one who had not grown up at home could have quite that accent. My new acquaintance introduced himself, and explained his presence. He and his brothers owned a large fruit orchard and farm in California, where he had lived since he was a boy. He had come back to India to pay a visit to some relatives who had lived near Hoshiapur for generations. He walked along beside us, and I was acutely aware of Sheila's discomfiture at our being so informally accosted by a strange man, whose antecedents were unknown. My new acquaintance was so obviously thrilled to find someone who was not only an American, but a Californian besides, that I felt almost sorry for him. He told me about his beautiful farm and his large fruit crop, and how rich the soil was and how comfortable his home. As he talked his voice was full of pride and longing for our homeland, and his eyes looked at the scene around us with pity and distaste. "It has been so long," he said. "I have not been back here for twenty years. But it never seems to change any. My people here do not believe me when I tell them about America." I felt that in some odd way he was even more an alien than I. Then he suddenly seemed to realize that though for two displaced Americans to greet each other with pleasure might be understandable by our standards, by Indian standards it was unthinkable for a stranger to "pick up" two high-class ladies. So we shook hands and said goodbye. Sheila was still embarrassed by the encounter, and obviously did not want to speak about it, so we walked on in silence. I could not help feeling that the lack of a common background puts a heavy burden on friendship.

I often think that the Indians I know best frequently forget when they are with me that our nationalities are different, and somehow do not like to be reminded. As soon as I know people at all, they become acquaintances, or friends or familiar faces, and I never think about their nationality or their color. This sometimes leads to an informality of behavior that can be misunderstood. I always remember a little story I was told about a small white boy in a racially mixed neighborhood who was having a birthday party. He informed his mother that he had invited all his best school friends to his party, and out of curiosity she asked, "Are any of your friends Negroes?" The little boy looked puzzled for a moment, then brightened, "I don't know, Mommie," he said, "I'll look at them tomorrow." And this is the way it should always be, not a proudly proclaimed tolerance, but a child's acceptance of people as they are, unconscious of the superficial differences that too often cloak our common humanity. As I forget the small differences that exist between my friends and me, so they must forget too at times. Then a chance word or expression labels me "American," and then I am no longer just me, but a white skin, a memory of years of arrogance, and a stranger who may ridicule or pity their country and its customs.

It is unfair, but true, that we Americans must share with all Europeans the burden of centuries of colonialism in which we played no part. To people in this area of the world, our white skins condemn us. We are guilty along with those who ruled them and controlled their destinies for so many years. For an American, proud of his country's record, this feeling of being blamed is sometimes unbearable. You want to shout, "It was not us. Why must you condemn us too?" But it is no use. Indians are absurdly naïve about the differences between Americans and English, and since they are at least accustomed to the English, and since we are richer, they sometimes dislike us more. It has often amused me, when I was with well bred Indians doing their utmost to be more British than the British, to think that I could probably find more Americans who hated the English than I could find Indians who hated them. Whether we like it or not we are guilty by association, and each individual American in the East must work as best he can to exonerate his country and uphold her ideals.

I did not mention my chance encounter with the American-Indian again. I felt Sheila was all too aware that he and I shared a common knowledge of a way of life she could never fully understand. We had shut her out. And for awhile I was to her an American, and she was an Indian. East was East and West was West and the curtain of race and nationality floated between us. But we joined Dr. Babbar and the curtain gradually faded away, and I became just Carol again.

Dr. Babbar offered to take me through the district hospital here, a sister hospital to ours. I was delighted with the chance, so we started on a busman's holiday. As we walked toward the hospital, the flies increased in number, though I would have thought that was an impossibility. The doctor hates flies with a ferocity which makes me very glad I do not have wings, and he treated us to a continual monologue on the filth, stench and general unwholesomeness of this town. He was not deterred by a foreigner's courtesy and he damned it so roundly with every step that Sheila and I exchanged amused glances. I will not describe the hospital. I do not think anyone would believe me. Ours, by comparison, seemed a haven of cleanliness and comfort. The dirt, the flies, the faces, the stained, putrid bandages were all horrible. One thing really shocked me. I noticed many amputation cases, and we have very few. I asked Dr. Babbar why there was this difference, and he spoke to the dispenser who was on duty. When he answered the question with so much violence, I knew he was as stunned as I. "They were all compound fractures," he said. "Good Lord, Carol, they amputate all their compound fractures!" The hospital was not as crowded as ours, which is now jammed with more beds than seems possible. After seeing this, I think I know better why people walk so many tired miles to reach us.

I was quiet when we left the hospital, and Dr. Babbar felt compelled to apologize and explain why though we have so little this hospital has so much less. He told me the pathetically small number of qualified surgeons who practice in all of the Punjab, he reminded me of the money we bully and beg from the Red Cross and the Americans to buy our medicines, and he explained the understandably low standards of some Indian doctors who are often trained in hospitals as dirty and primitive as this. Our hospital is rich. We are well supplied by any but western standards, because in Nangal there are a group of American advisers who are insistent that a good doctor and hospital facilities be provided if they are to remain. For a year I have been envious of all that the hospitals at home contain that is lacking here. I have watched children die, and known that they would have lived in America. Now I feel guilty that our Indian hospital is taking the bigger share here. For our patients we demand all that we can beg, borrow or steal; we want the best available, and get it, perhaps at the expense of this little hospital and others like it. If we used less penicillin there might be more here to stop the infections that made those amputations necessary. Medical care for Indians and Americans is free in Nangal, and the money must be procured somehow to pay for it all. I wonder how much longer it will be necessary to save one life at the cost of another. I wonder how thin help can be spread. I wonder if I will be able to control myself the next time someone comes to our hospital and demands penicillin for a fever of ninety-nine degrees and a runny nose!

We ended our day searching for a restaurant less fly-ridden than most, so that we could eat dinner before starting back to Nangal. We finally found one which looked at least clean, but we were so hungry by that time it could have been pretty bad before discouraging us. Dr. Babbar went in first, strode back to the kitchen, looked it over and motioned us to enter. The owner fluttered around us in a perfect imitation of a French headwaiter. He bowed and salaamed us to seats, showed us an open faucet where we could wash, and scurried off to cook our curry. I was amused by his behavior, but Sheila and Dr. Babbar were hilarious. As soon as he had left us, the two of them began to laugh, and refused to tell me what the joke was. After I had said, "For Pete's sake, tell me what is so funny," a dozen times or so, the doctor relented and explained. It seems the restaurant owner believed Dr. Babbar was a Moslem, and Sheila and I were his two wives. Since it is well known that European wives are an expensive luxury, he had decided the doctor must be a maharajah of some sort, traveling incognito. He had even seen fit to compliment the doctor on his young wife's white skin. I was as entertained as they, and we did our best not to disappoint the little man by behaving as we thought a disguised maharajah and his harem should under the circumstances.

fifteen

This is the most crowded summer we have had yet at the hospital. Dr. Babbar had a graph drawn by one of the draftsmen here to show the increase in patients since the hospital's beginning. This graph with its little line going up, up, up each year shows better than numbers can how much we have gained the confidence of the villagers, and what a burden of patients we are carrying. The hot months and the monsoon seasons always bring us our heaviest load, but last year was nothing compared to this. Even the small bed in my newly acquired office was pressed into service, and then there were no more. The staff held a meeting and requested that no more patients be admitted. The other doctors explained to their Chief that we had so many cases now that they were working hours of overtime every day and running out of medicine. We have no more beds, no more linen; the crowded conditions and the overworked staff make any attempt at cleanliness very difficult; the flies are increasing daily; we have so many fever cases that it is difficult to keep them separated; it gets hotter every day, and still people keep coming. I knew what Dr. Babbar's answer would be before they petitioned him, and I was not disappointed. "We are going to admit every single patient who comes to us requiring hospitalization," he said. "Anyone whom you would have admitted before, you must admit now. They are better off lying on the floor where we can give them some treatment, than dying on the road with nothing. I don't care how much overtime you all work. I expect every member of the staff to stay on duty until the work is done, no matter how long that is, and I will do the same." Then he softened his voice. "I know how hard you are all working, and I understand the problems, but we must just keep going somehow until the worst is past." Then back to fire and brimstone, "Let me tell you, if I find that one single serious case has been refused admission I will personally strangle the doctor involved. I will excuse the Assistant Surgeon from all operations and Harnam Singh the dispenser, and Sister Carol can assist in the theater, but don't stop admitting opera-tive cases. We can operate at night if we can't find time in the day. And if any of you permit one single septic case to get into the surgical ward, that person will wash bedpans for a month!" Then back to honey, "I am grateful for all of you, and I have complete confidence in your ability to handle any situation. Now let's stop wasting time and go back to work." Everyone left, some grumbling, some cowed, and he started in on me.

"Sister," he used my newly acquired honorary title, "phone the housing office and tell them we must have more beds, any kind, but find some. Tell all the nurses to inform new patients that we have no bedding for them; they will have to use their own. Phone the Public Health Officer and tell him we have too much typhoid. He must find out where these cases are coming from, and do something about the well water. Make him send us a team of DDT men, and see that the hospital is sprayed, every inch of it. Call the dhobis in and tell them we must have the laundry back in a shorter time or I will fire all of them. You must get some more money from the Americans. We are running out of medicine. Tell them we have too much typhoid and typhus, and must have more Chloromycetin. Try to get them to send more eggs too. Tell the Indian Red Cross ladies they must send us extra milk, and some kind of fruitade. We have too many patients getting dehydrated, and we will not have enough glucose saline for all of them. I sent a case of smallpox to the isolation hut by the river this morning. Send one of the sweepers to take care of him, and remind me to go and see him later. See if you can fit one more bed into each ward. Try to get all the typhoid cases together in one place. Move all the septic cases onto the far veranda. Call that labor representative and tell him we need some food. See if any of the Americans can send us ice a couple of times a day for the fever cases. Tell Sundar to have the operation theater ready twenty-four hours a day. Tell him if he runs out of sterilized linen to wash it himself. Get some fly swatters. I want you to give a fly swatter and an empty matchbox to every patient who can swing his arm. Tell them they must kill a hundred flies a day, and if they don't fill the matchboxes with flies I will be angry. Tell them this is called 'occupational therapy'! Remind me this afternoon to order more A.T.S. serum. Find out how much typhoid vaccine we have and tell the staff to start lining up at three o'clock. I want everyone to get a booster shot." He paused, "Keep an eye on the outpatient clinic and let me know if they are not admitting people. Come and get me if any case comes in that looks serious. The other doctors are so busy they may not get around to some of them in time. Tell the nurses I want a fluid chart kept on every fever case, and on every patient who is dehydrated on admission." He finally stopped. I had filled four pages in my notebook, and was trying to decide which things should come first. Then he finished. "Well, I guess that is all for now. Come back in a hour or so when you have finished, and I will tell you some more." I went out into the hall to laugh, and wished with all my heart that some of the Americans who wonder what I do when I hang around the hospital all day could have heard my instructions.

The ladies of the Indian Red Cross have come up with a marvelous idea. They have got together and organized a mobile medical unit, with Sheila Babbar for doctor, to go several times a week to two of the larger outlying villages. In this way we can treat many of the less serious cases at their own doorsteps, and take some of the burden from the hospital. Sheila asked me to come along and do the dressings part of the time, and I agreed to go with them for their first trip at least. Our supplies are rather limited, but we have quinine, sulfa drugs, and cod-liver oil and liver tonics for the children. On the first morning we were late getting started because we couldn't remember whether we had packed enough cotton and had taken the thermometer, but finally we all crowded into our conveyance— an old British Army jeep which had been enclosed to make a sort of station wagon. By the time the six of us and our boxes of antiseptics, medicines and bandages had been jammed in, there was hardly room for the driver. I felt again, as I looked at my companions, that I would never understand upper-class Indian women. There they were, going out to do social work in the villages, and every one of them, except Sheila and myself, was dressed in a lovely sari and wearing elaborate jewelry. It seems hardly tactful to parade your own wealth so ostentatiously when you are trying to assist people who have nothing.

Our bus swayed and stuttered along the narrow road that edges one of the canals, for nearly ten miles, then turned off onto a rutted trail which gradually turned into a dried creek bed. We twisted along, bumping with dreadful lurches over rocks and boulders, trying to keep our bottles from breaking, and our heads from hitting the roof every time we jolted. I had just about resigned myself to being very sick when we pulled up at our destination. The "Mayor" of the village knew we were coming and had prepared a small first-aid station for us. It was a one-room hut with a large open porch. But it had been whitewashed and swept clean, so it looked quite presentable. We set up three tables on the porch, one for Sheila to use, one for medicines and one for dressings and bandages. We unloaded the jeep and started arranging our supplies, while each of us wondered whether there was any point in continuing, since only a few children with thumbs in their mouths and a pack of stray dogs seemed interested in our activities. Patients were notable only by their absence. Shortly an excited man appeared and talked to Sheila for a few minutes, then shouted to some little boys and ran off. Sheila explained that people had come from many of the surrounding villages before dawn that morning to see us, but when we were late they had given up hope and drifted off to lie in the shade. The man had sent the children to spread the word that we had finally arrived, and in a few minutes people started to collect around our makeshift clinic, until there was an unbelievable mob.

Sheila sat at her table and, assisted by another lady, examined, diagnosed, and sent patients either on to me to have eyes or ears cleaned, cuts bandaged or abscesses dressed, or on to the medicine table to have a prescription filled. Each patient carried his own bottle for medicines, usually stoppered by a piece of dried corncob. The pills we wrapped in bits of newspaper. Once we got started I scarcely looked up to see what the others were doing. It was so hot, and the people were packed around us so closely, that I could hardly breathe. I washed eyes and cleaned the maggots out of draining ears. I bandaged cuts and poured sulfa powder on open boils, and I did it all in a kind of daze, hardly seeing whom I was working on. The only respite was to wash my hands in the pail of water at my feet, and dry them on my skirt. Eventually I would notice that the water was getting dirtier and bloodier with each hand washing, and shout for a boy to dump it out and bring me a clean bucket from the well. I tried to remember to pour alcohol over my hands between patients, but we soon were short of antiseptic and I could not even do that. The only patients I remember clearly were the several I felt we should take back to the hospital. One of these was a tiny girl whose head was completely covered with an enormous abscess. She was running a high fever and seemed desperately ill. I told Sheila that this child, at least, we must take back to Nangal, but she only laughed and said, "She is not as sick as you think." It took me an hour to clean the child's head with hydrogen peroxide and alcohol. There was not an inch of healthy skin on her whole skull. The whole mess was dripping pus and matted with ashes and dung. I knew my efforts to clean it must hurt, but the baby was so sick and apathetic, she hardly moved. I kept thinking, "This one has got to have penicillin. She probably has malaria too. This will never be enough to help her." But Sheila was the doctor, and in the end we gave her sulfa pills and quinine and a rich tonic of iron, vitamins and cod-liver oil. I poured sulfa powder all over her head, and wrapped it tightly with a huge bandage like a helmet. Then I threatened her mother with a dire fate if she so much as touched the bandage or tried to peek underneath it. I certainly did not want to have to clean the whole mess again next week.

We worked for hours without stopping, and I knew the others must be as exhausted and hot as I. Finally the mob thinned out to a trickle, and since our medicines were mostly gone we finished up the few stragglers and promised to bring more and come again in six days. I felt I would give anything to lie down on the ground under the mango tree and just smoke a cigarette. But this was not to be. To show their gratitude the richest man in the village had prepared refreshments for us, so we picked our way through the streets to his house. My hair and clothes were soaking wet with perspiration. The flies walked around on my face and I was too tired to brush them away. We finally sat down to a table on the veranda and our host proudly passed a tray of ripe bananas and poured us each a glass of lemonade. The bananas were all right, but when I tasted the lemonade I thought I would never be able to swallow it. The stuff was warm and sickeningly sweet, and floating through it was a heavy deposit of dirt and grit. Later Sheila told me most of it was pepper and spices, but it *looked* like dirt. All the messy jobs I had been working on suddenly hit my usually cast-iron stomach, and it rolled over and over, while I tried to tell myself that I could not possibly permit myself to be sick here. The others were having a difficult problem with their drinks too. I could see that no one wanted even to taste it. But they had more freedom to be rude than I. I tried to keep thinking of how proudly this treat had been given us and how hurt the villagers would be if all of us left it untouched, and little by little I got most of it down. I felt quite sure I would end up with cholera, typhoid and dysentery, but I could not bear to let these people know that their best was not good enough.

When I got home Ram followed me around the house scolding. He even shouted at me through the bathroom door while I showered. "Mem-sahib-ji, where you been? You been out in the sun again? What you been doing? You look bad. You been working too hard? Mem-sahib-ji, you been with some bad sick peoples again? You lay down on bed right now! You not home for lunch. You eat lunch already? I go fix something." I could hear him through the wall grumbling and crashing dishes. By the time I had scrubbed my hair, stood under the cold shower, and put on some lipstick, I felt human again. But it was necessary to pacify Ram by lying down. I put on a house-coat, and reclined gracefully among the cushions while he brought my lunch on a tray. My meek acceptance of his orders gratified him. He loves to see me sitting around doing nothing. That is the way mem-sahibs are supposed to behave! I was dying to go over to the hospital to see what had happened there during my absence. But Ram was standing over me watching every mouthful, and I knew if I left again he would tell Bart. In fact he would make such a good story that Bart would be convinced that I had collapsed twenty miles away, been carried home on a stretcher and had a blood transfusion. I wonder if Ram knows I am pregnant. He probably knew a month before I did.

sixteen

Before I ever leave the United States again I am going to find out how much milk American cows give. Every Indian I have met here sooner or later asks me that question. They find it quite incomprehensible that I have no idea, and have never given the subject much thought. In fact, I believe I will have a mimeographed list drawn up which reads:

1. American cows give an average of ? gallons milk per day.
2. No, I have never seen a lynching.
3. The War in Korea was a United Nations action which we supported in conjunction with *several other countries*.
4. Yes, I am aware that the United States engineered a revolution in Panama to ensure construction and control of the Panama Canal.
5. Yes, I believe that both Alaska and Hawaii should be admitted to statehood. Yes, the reason that Hawaii has not been admitted is partly because of racial prejudice, but there are other reasons.
6. The United States does not send all its surplus food to underprivileged countries because it would completely disrupt their economies, and because it would cost the American people millions of dollars to transport.

7. No, I do not think that either *Grapes of Wrath* or *Tobac-co Road* gives a representative picture of life in America.
8. I am sorry, but there is absolutely no way in which I could help you to emigrate to the United States.

The last statement should be in italics. The amazing thing to me is that so few poorer-class Indians ever inquire about the possibility of getting into our country. It is usually the well-to-do Indian who wants to emigrate, and most frequently a young man who has prefaced his request with an hour-long dissertation on what a materialistic, racially prejudiced, dishonest, selfish, imperialistic, thoroughly impossible country we are!

I think the questions about our racial prejudice annoy me most. I do not see how Indians, who are the most color-conscious people I have ever met, feel that they can even bring up the subject. I have lived in the South, and I never met a southerner who carried his racial discrimination as far as 95 per cent of the Indians do. Indian standards of beauty are based on the degree of lightness of the skin. Their caste and class-consciousness are mostly a matter of skin color. Even the first question they ask when a baby is born is not, "Is it healthy?" or "Is it a boy?" but rather, *"How light is it?"* I know because I have heard them. Yet they consider us prejudiced! Many well educated young Indians are, or pretend to be, naïvely convinced that lynchings are a common occurrence in every town in America. It is almost pointless to argue with people like this, but if you refuse to discuss these subjects, they assume it is because they are correct in their misconceptions. It would be easy if Americans could honestly deny such allegations categorically, but unfortunately we cannot. We have to admit that racial discrimination is a problem in the United States—a problem we are trying to solve gradually by democratic means—while still refuting their absurd ideas about its extent and degree. I have spent hours trying to explain the economic and social reasons for racial discrimination in America, reasons which do exist whether I, personally, like it or not, only to have my Indian acquaintance remain convinced that I am concealing the true facts.

I feel that no American overseas should ever apologize for our country or our people. It is not necessary that we claim perfection for our country. One reason we love America is because we have the freedom to criticize and disagree with certain conditions which exist there. We have made mistakes in the past, we will undoubtedly make mistakes in the future. Every country does. The fact that Americans are permitted to acknowledge these mistakes publicly is unmistakable evidence that we enjoy the personal liberty we claim. I do not mind answering absurd charges or discussing American attitudes. I can even agree that our country has not always behaved with exemplary righteousness on every occasion. But I see no necessity for ever feeling shame for America, or for apologizing in any way for what we are. There is nothing wrong about making mistakes. There is nothing wrong about having problems. We are, after all, human. We can feel proud of our country and love the ideals she stands for, although aware of her imperfections. There, surely, is our strength. Some Americans try to buy friendship for themselves and their country by continually apologizing for her. There is a great deal of difference between explaining and admitting mistakes about America and ridiculing or apologizing for our way of life. It is very easy to buy personal popularity by these means in India, unfortunately, and a few succumb to the temptation. It is frequently the more intellectual, cultured American who makes this mistake. Such people apparently wish to disassociate themselves from the less admirable of our national traits, to prove that they, at least, are cultivated, educated and discriminating. To do so they are willing to ridicule American "vulgarity," to speak with amused tolerance of American "mass culture" and to give everyone the impression that they find little to admire in their country. Americans like this will do far more harm to us, in the long run, than any number of rude, gum-chewing tourists.

The problem of answering Indian critics of the United States is made more difficult by the fact that many of them seem to have been given an extensive education in American history as it would be taught by someone who despised America. Sometimes the source of this adverse propaganda is all too evident. It is not hard to refute ridiculous misconceptions and absurd charges when they are made by someone obviously ignorant of his subject. But it is trying indeed to reply to a critic who rattles off dates and episodes from our past that most of us know little or nothing about. I think I have as good a background in American history as most, but when I am challenged, for instance, to give an explanation for our manipulation of politics in a South American country in 1911, I am at a complete loss. I wish our State Department would issue a comprehensive American history for its citizens abroad which would have as its purpose a frank appraisal of some of the less admirable incidents in our history, and the reasons for them, along with facts and figures which can be used to deny the charges made against us. Then we could argue intelligently with our detractors, and not be in the embarrassing position of having to admit our ignorance on so many little known points.

There is one criticism of our country that I encourage with great glee, certain of my ability to provide an iron-clad rebuttal. The young Indian intellectuals who make most of these charges against us sooner or later start talking about the treatment given to the American Indian. I let them rave on about our cruelty in depriving our Indians of their homeland, and admit that there are black marks against us for parts of our past in this respect. I even agree that certain Indian tribes today are among our most underprivileged citizens. This, however, is seldom satisfaction enough for most Indian debaters. They go on and on, charging passionately that our American Indians are prisoners on their barren reservations, miserable and starving.

There I have them! It happens that several of the Americans
who have worked here are either full-blooded or half-blooded
American Indians. So I can reply to my tormentor, "Oh, is that
so? They are all starving in concentration camps, are they? Well
in that case how about Mr. So-and-so? He was an American
Indian you know. Why don't you go talk to Mrs. Blank? Her
father and brother own quite a large sheep ranch on a reserva-
tion. She could probably tell you much more about American
Indians than I can." It gives me pleasure to see the chagrin and
confusion on the face of my challenger and to force him to
admit that many of our Indians are ordinary citizens, indis-
tinguishable from the rest of us. I only wish we had American
Negroes working here too.

The other morning when I opened my front door, I found
little Nita and her mother both asleep on the veranda. It has
been six months since Nita left the hospital, and we had heard
nothing about her. I long ago decided that we would never see
her again. I was happy to find that she was still alive and I could
hardly believe it. I woke them both up and had Ram make them
some tea while I talked to them. Nita's mother was dreadfully
upset. She was afraid that we would not let Nita come back to
the hospital because she had taken her away without our permission. Nita looked terrible. Her condition has deteriorated a
great deal during these months she has been gone, but she is as
sweet as ever. She clutched my skirt in both hands as we walked
up to the hospital. I got her back into the children's ward and
put to bed. I only hope we can help her at least a little.

I heard the most uncanny story this morning. It was told by
a village woman who came into the hospital for treatment. I
am putting it down exactly as it was translated for me.
"About five years ago, I dreamed one night that a large black

cobra had bitten me on the hand as I drew water from the well. The dream was so real that I awoke in terror. For two days after the dream I felt feverish and ill. On the third day I went to the well for water, and as I put my hand down, a large cobra struck it, just as it had happened in my dream. I had told of my dream to many, and the people in my village were much amazed by the occurrence. My hand became much swollen and very red, and I was very sick for many days. But finally I became well again.

"Nothing happened for one year, then again I dreamed of the snake. I was much frightened this time and did not go to the well for many days. I thought I had waited until the danger was over, but when I did finally go for water, again the snake was there, and bit me on the arm. Six months later the whole thing happened again. Since that time the dreams have been coming closer and closer together. Now the snake bites me every two or three months. It is no longer always at the well, but sometimes in the fields or near the house. I always have the dream several days beforehand and now I am so filled with fear that I am afraid to go to sleep at night. I think that this snake must be a curse upon me, and that someday he will finally kill me. Six days ago again he struck, and this time my husband has brought me here to see if your medicine has power over this dream."

As proof of her story she showed us her hands and arms. They were dotted with fang marks; some were old and indistinct, but the most recent were angry and raw. Her husband, the village schoolmaster, confirmed what she had told us.

Dr. Babbar admitted her to the wards for observation, then we spent an interesting hour going over her story. The doctor felt that she was a neurotic woman who was deliberately inflicting wounds on herself to gain attention, but he confessed that the marks on her arm looked exactly like those made by a cobra, and was puzzled as to how she could make them swell so readily. I lean towards the theory that there really is a snake, and that it really does strike her. Perhaps she has a particular odor that attracts it. She could have built up an immunity to the snake venom over the years, and surely it is not surprising that she dreams about cobras. I am sure if I were bitten I would dream of nothing else. Whatever the explanation of her story, she was certainly deeply afraid, and I am glad that no snake is haunting me.

It seems impossible that the monsoons are here again. How quickly this year has passed. Now I am almost an old-timer in Nangal. I no longer love this place and these people because they are novel, but because they have become familiar and dear. Last year I found the monsoons exciting and dramatic. This year I have become so practical that almost my only reaction to their arrival is chagrin that the water is rising and our trips to the villages with the mobile clinic will soon be impossible. I have become an awful bore. My enthusiasm for the hospital, the patients, the staff and everything that happens there has gotten completely out of bounds. My friends, Indian and American, are quite sick of the subject, and I must say that I don't blame them. There is nothing more tiresome than a person with one consuming interest—unless that person happens to be you.

I have been dumbfounded at the amount that our little mobile clinic with its few medicines has been able to accomplish. One example of the effectiveness of our crude treatments is the little child with the head abscess. When I returned to the village six days after our first visit, I treated her again. I would not have known that it was the same baby if I had not recognized the bandage. Her fever was gone, her eyes were bright, she smiled at me, and best of all her head was almost completely healed. Sheila had the last word. "See, Carol," she said, "I told you she was not so sick!" We gave her more vitamins and cod-liver oil to take, and the last time I saw her she was playing about, almost plump. Of course we cannot really claim much credit. Sulfa works miracles out here where people have not had it before and its potency is undiminished.

The rush at the hospital during the past few months and the crowded urgency of each day have pushed me into attempting more and more new things. I am in charge of the linens now, and sometimes feel that I spend whole days simply counting dirty sheets. Every single piece of linen that is sent out to be washed must be counted when it goes, and counted when it comes back. If not, the men who wash it would gradually steal all we possess. The hospital has been expanding during these months and we now have an outdoor dining room and recreation room for the ambulatory patients and a physical therapy room with a small pool for water therapy. Mrs. Johti Syrup, one of the ladies of the Indian Red Cross, and one of the finest woman I have ever met, does most of our physical therapy, coming day after day to work with damaged hands or crippled legs. Most of what I do cannot be defined or placed in a neat category. I am just a glorified errand girl, and some times not even so glorified. I still get to know most of the patients and spend time in the wards, but since I became pregnant I have been less and less a social worker, and more and more an administrative assistant to Dr. Babbar.

seventeen

Yesterday we, and several thousand other people, spent the whole day with Prime Minister Nehru. The occasion was the pouring of the first bucket of concrete at Bhakra, with Mr. Nehru officiating. We were invited to the ceremony itself, a luncheon in his honor, and later a more formal dinner. Almost all the Americans attended the functions along with a great number of Indian engineers and assorted dignitaries. For days work at Bhakra has been slowing down to a standstill so that the job could be tidied and made more presentable. A dam under construction is a messy place at best, but every attempt was made to polish it up for company. Then, of course, they had to practice pouring concrete, so that when the time came to pour the "first" bucket it would all go smoothly.

Ram gloated for weeks over our invitations, even though I explained several times that we were not precisely the only people to receive them. The first bucket was to be dumped early in the morning, so even earlier we presented ourselves for his inspection, shoes polished, gloves on. Even the car had been diligently scrubbed by the sweeper and gardener all the day before. Just as Bart and I prepared to get in and drive off, Ram said, "One minute, Sahib," and dashed to his quarters. When he returned he had donned his official best hat. Made of astra-

137

kan, this monstrosity, moth-eaten and stained, is so large that it completely covers Ram's eyebrows and is held up only by his protruding ears. Ram, however, considers it the last word and brings it out only on the most formal occasions. "O.K., Sahib," Ram informed us, "we go now." "But Ram," we said in chorus, "you have to have an invitation. They won't let you come in." Ram drew himself up, gave one of his imperial shrugs, and reassured us, "It's O.K., Mem-sahib, I go too!" This seemed to be the end of the matter, so we all got in the car. Ram's bearing was so completely one of assured self-confidence that I spent the whole trip to Bhakra wondering if he had perhaps received a personal note from the Pandit requesting that he be on hand. Bart was nervous about the possible difficulties of trying to sneak our cook into such an eminent gathering, and kept muttering under his breath, "Never saw this man before, sir."

We arrived and parked the car. No one seemed to notice Ram, and we made our way together to the special tented platform where the speeches and ceremony were to be conducted. Ram gradually drifted ahead of us, and by the time we reached the roped off and guarded seats, he was already inside the enclosure chatting casually with some well garbed Hindus. Bart claims that he later saw the astrakan hat bobbing around on the speaker's dais.

The Punjab Police Band, a magnificent group of bearded Sikhs dressed in a combination of turbans and Scotch plaids, entertained us with bagpipe music until the Prime Minister and his party arrived. Then the speeches began. Since they were all in Hindi we had plenty of time to look around, and to appreciate just how cold we were. The wind was whistling up through Bhakra gorge, and though the sun was out, we were all seated in deep shade. Covering the hills and rocks around us were crowds of workmen and their families. They were grouped in utter silence straining to hear the words of the speeches which drifted out to them over the loud-speaker. There was the usual dull assortment before the Prime Minister's speech. When he finally rose and took his place before the microphone an even deeper hush was noticeable. Mr. Nehru spoke in Hindi also, but with what a difference! Even though the words were unknown to us, it was impossible to remain unmoved by his voice and his compelling delivery. He made small jokes, and appreciative laughter drifted back to us from the people on the abutments. He bowed his head and spoke with deep emotion, and other heads bowed too. I was following his speech in a written translation: he was not saying anything particularly original, but the way he said it made the words important. All of us who had never seen him before had been surprised when he entered at his almost frail smallness. But it was impossible to think of him as a little man when he spoke. He has an actor's gift of giving the illusion of height by sheer force of personality.

It was after the speeches were finished that Mr. Nehru did something that endeared him to all the American construction men present. I am certain he did not realize how much he pleased us, or how much we were impressed by an action that seemed totally spontaneous on his part. He was to pour officially the first bucket of concrete, and to do so made his way, with the dignitaries of the party, down a long zigzag trail to the very depths of the gorge. The American crane operator swung out and lowered the concrete bucket down and down, very slowly. Everyone expected that the Prime Minister would simply touch the bucket, or merely stand by as it was poured. Instead, as the concrete reached him, he grasped the busting rod firmly, and using it skillfully busted the bucket himself. Had this been a gathering solely of Americans, Mr. Nehru would have been promptly pounded on the back, and given a good rousing cheer. As it was, from all around I could hear Americans muttering in hushed tones, "Well, I'll be damned. He busted the bucket!" "Bucket busting" is a dirty job. We are all so accustomed to the well bred Hindus' complete distaste for any kind of physical labor that Mr. Nehru's performance was an exciting indication

that some high-placed Indians at least were not averse to soil-
ing their hands. He not only soiled his hands, he spattered concrete on himself and his party with complete nonchalance.

We drove back hurriedly from the first function in order to
have time to change for the second, the luncheon to be given
in Nangal. Ram was pensive in the car, but admitted that the
speeches had been quite satisfactory. He disappeared as soon
as we reached home, and Bart suggested that he probably was
on some sort of private errand for the Governor. The luncheon
was held out of doors in what had been, the day before, a barren field. Now it was transformed with flower pots, tinkling
fountains and very bright tentlike hangings called shamianas.
The field had been divided almost in half. On one side were
the more elaborate rugs, furniture, and tables for the official
party and the important few; on the other the rest of us were
to eat in less magnificence. The food was delicious. We joined
our Indian friends the Lambas, and Dr. and Mrs. Babbar, and
consumed quantities of chicken tanduri, and the puffy bread
called nan, with our fingers. We were all curious to catch a
closer look at the Prime Minister, but ranged along the line
dividing our two enclosures were several little men intent on
keeping back the herd. No one was particularly upset by these
arrangements. None of us had precisely expected to jog elbows
with Mr. Nehru while eating, and it seems only fair that a public
figure be permitted to down a chicken leg in at least compara-
tive privacy now and then. But Mr. Nehru did not share this
point of view. About halfway through the luncheon he became
aware that a certain segregation was being enforced. As I heard
later from a friend who had infiltrated nearby, he made known
his disapproval of the arrangement in no uncertain terms. And
shortly we saw the Prime Minister cross the dividing line himself and come over to share our more humble appointments.
He wandered about through the crowd of several thousand,
stopping now and then to chat with different ones, and even to
nibble from a plate of food hastily provided for him. The quak-

ing officials in charge of the affair followed him apologetically, but except for an occasional glance of withering disapproval he ignored them altogether.

After the luncheon, Dr. Babbar and I hastened back to the hospital to get it ready for inspection. The daughter of the Governor had informed us of her intention to visit it, and we wanted to be prepared. The Governor's daughter acts as his official hostess, and I have met her several times at receptions and teas in her honor given whenever she visited Nangal. I have never ceased to be impressed with her beauty. This amuses my Indian friends who do not find her flamboyant enough to be beautiful by Indian standards. She is a slight little thing, and dresses with taste and simplicity. The ladies of the Indian Red Cross soon joined us at the hospital and skittered about distributing a piece of fruit to each of the patients with firm instructions that it was to be prominently displayed and under no circumstances to be eaten until our visitor had departed. (This used to annoy me past endurance, and their custom of passing out toys to the bedridden children and then collecting them the moment the visitor leaves, still does. However, they seem so innocent of the hypocrisy involved; the patients get to eat the fruit eventually, and the children have toys for a few minutes anyway, so I suppose no harm is done by the pretense.) The inspection of the hospital by the Governor's daughter and her entourage was completed without a hitch, and I went home to rest and change for the dinner party that night.

The dinner was a more exclusive affair, limited to a few hundred people, Americans and Indians. It was held in the same tented compound, which looked even more oriental and opulent under the sparse electric lights. We dined amply on well prepared food and I wondered again at the difficulties involved in serving and cooking the food for these large gatherings with no more than charcoal fires available. Each of us was presented to Mr. Nehru separately, and he mingled with the crowd through the long evening, growing frailer and more weary before our eyes. He had traveled two hundred and fifty miles that morning to reach the dam, and would make the same drive back to New Delhi that night. I think most of us wished that someone would have sense enough to end his ordeal and allow him the rest he so obviously needed. Finally, his eyes almost glazed with fatigue, he left. The long day was over.

eighteen

I am getting lazier and lazier. I had to stop going to the villages and bouncing over those rocky roads. Even at the hospital I find myself looking around for a place to sit. The ether makes me wobbly in the operating theater, and one of the little sweepers there hovers behind me with a three-legged stool, waiting for a sign. It is not as though there weren't many months left, alas!

I did the most stupid thing the other day. Dim memories of articles I had read and taken seriously with my first baby filtered back, and I decided that I really should do something about my appearance. As I recall, it is important to take extra pains with hair and face. I took pains all right—no one is even going to notice my waistline for at least six months. My hair seemed to present the gravest problem since the part of it that is bleached by the sun was sticking out in all directions, and the part that is not seemed to have simply given up in despair. I hunted around in the bazaar and found a nice fat bottle of black hair dye, and shut myself into the bathroom with it. Anyone would have sense enough to consider that there might be a slight difference between our hair rinses and black Indian dye, but I was so enthusiastic about the whole project that I just dove in and, with the aid of a toothbrush, started slathering it on. It was black all right and my hair absorbed it nicely; so did my ears, neck, forehead, hands and any other spot that caught a drip. Worst of all, my eyebrows looked so anemic compared to the rest of me that I decided to do them also. When I finally ran out of dye I had achieved a unique combination of Carmen Miranda and John L. Lewis. I decided then to wash off the excess. The excess did not wash off. Soap did not remove it, nor did lemon juice. The bottle said "everlasting black" and it certainly seemed to live up to its advertising. I got more and more frantic, and every glance in the mirror confirmed the seriousness of my predicament. Finally I yelled through the door for Ram to go get my next-door neighbor quickly. Helen is absolutely the best neighbor in the world, and has never been known to let any emergency intimidate her. She arrived, took one look at me, and started laughing. I laughed too, but my amusement had certain bitter overtones. Helen found a bottle of ammonia and managed to control her hilarity enough to scrub me. By the time the ammonia fumes had nearly blinded both of us, my ears and neck had dimmed to a deep walnut brown. The rest will just have to wear off. My brows still meet in the middle with a grim scowl, and my hands appear to be forever encased in dark gloves, but as I said, no one is going to notice my waistline. To add insult to injury, my hair has a certain green tinge in the sunlight which gives it a mildewed appearance I had hardly intended.

The children are voting halfheartedly for a girl. I think they know as well as I that it is to be another boy. The question of names will be a problem. Tony is greatly enamored of a little girl here named Roberta, and insists that this is the only name fit for a girl. Steve is studying mythology in school, and is just as determined that his new sister be called either Pandora or Venus. A wandering fortuneteller cornered me the other day, and foretold that I was to have three more children—all girls. I was unable to take his palm reading too seriously, since he prophesied a boy for a friend who had had a hysterectomy ten years ago.

Bart has bought a jeep and now spends every spare moment hunting. There is a great deal of game here, but most of the men are primarily interested in the nilgai, a very large antelope which we use for meat. They also hunt wild pig, peacock, deer, and leopard. We are careful to shoot the peacocks only in certain areas where the villagers approve, since in other places the birds are protected and killing them is unwise. The rest of the game can be hunted almost everywhere. Before coming to India we were warned that people did not appreciate having the nilgai hunted, since many regarded it as a close relative of the cow, which it is not. Bart did not hunt for a long time because of these warnings, but they turned out to be another example of how little upper-class Indians understand their village brothers. Far from disliking us to hunt the country, most villagers encourage it, sending runners into town to bring news of the presence of a herd and, as we drive through the countryside, stopping us to plead that we shoot in their area. It is not a sporting matter to these Indians, but sheer self-preservation. In one night a herd of these animals can lay waste the crops of a whole village. Guns and ammunition are carefully regulated here, and of course expensive. It is a rare village that owns as much as an ancient twenty-two. Some of the Sikh villagers do hunt with these, and even have trained dogs, a species something like a greyhound, to help them, but for most of the people there is no defense possible against the ravaging animals.

It is surprising how few of our Indian friends believe us when we tell them of the villagers' eagerness to greet our hunters, and even fewer of them can bring themselves to believe that many of these people also eat the meat. Frequently we are asked to leave one of the animals behind when we have killed two, which seems to prove that what you will eat depends upon how hungry you are. To us, the meat has become a staple part of our diet, replacing goat meat. Nilgai is a very lean venison with a rich flavor, and many of us think it is superior to beef. We butcher the animals ourselves, cutting off steaks and roasts for our own use, and distributing the rest to Americans who do not hunt or are out of meat. Some of our Indian friends will also eat it, and what is left is frequently used by the servants. I have also fed the meat to patients at the hospital, with their full permission.

The nilgai hunts take all night and sometimes cover hundreds of miles, so I do not go. The wild pig hunts are less arduous and lots of fun for me. Usually we go with another American couple just across the river. The men conceal themselves along a path where the villagers say the pigs go for water, while Dee and I sit comfortably in the jeep and visit. All of this is done at night, which adds to our enjoyment. We sit in the dark surrounded by utter silence. Around us the leaves rustle and the air is full of the rich scent of wild marigolds. The village men sleep all night in their fields when the crops have come up, to protect them from the animals. Soon we can hear one of these farmers, far away, calling out in alarm and rattling his warning device of tins and sticks. A nearer farmer takes up his call, and soon it echoes and reechoes from the countryside around us.

I did go with Bart to a village a hundred miles from here where he hunts for black buck. We went as the guests of Dr. and Sheila Babbar, since the village is one where Sheila practiced during the war, when Dr. Babbar was serving with the British army. This village is the home of a large school for village girls which has an interesting history. About twenty-five years ago, one of the farmers in the village lost his only son, and shortly after, his only daughter was made a widow. The farmer was an old man, and he began to worry about what would happen to his daughter when he died, with no brother or husband to look after her. He finally concluded that the only thing that could possibly help her in her situation was an education. He was illiterate himself, as was nearly everyone in the village, but he became increasingly convinced that all the village girls should be educated so that they would never be in his daughter's position. So in his own home he started a school, hiring one teacher. His daughter was the first to graduate, and she at once started teaching also. The villagers nearby began to send their daughters to the tiny school, and, as more became educated, they in turn became teachers. The school became larger and larger over the years, as girls from villages far away were sent to learn. The farmer continued to grow their food, and his wife did the cooking. Tuition was less than a dollar a month. Now they have several buildings, including a college and a small hospital, all run on a sort of cooperative basis by the villagers. There are about seven hundred girls attending. The old farmer and his wife are dead, but their daughter has continued the work, and is now in charge of the project. All this has been accomplished by the people themselves in a tiny mud-walled place without electricity or even running water.

When we arrived it was dark and the girls were all studying, seated with their books around kerosene lanterns. Hundreds of peacocks strutted about screaming at us and fanning their tails proudly. Pye-dogs and jackals slunk around in the shadows snarling and fighting. First we were given the opportunity to refresh ourselves with a bath. I stood in a tub and poured dipperfuls of cold well water over myself, feeling it was one of the most enjoyable baths I had ever taken. Then we sat down to a really magnificent Indian meal, which had been cooked in a cubicle over a small open fire. Each dish was delicious and we ate and ate, enjoying both the food and the company of several teachers. For the Babbars it was a reunion with old friends, but they were careful to see that we were included.

After dinner we were shown our sleeping place. Native beds had been set up in the open courtyard of one of the village houses. Peacocks roosted in the trees over our heads, and a few feet away two buffaloes shared our accommodations, chewing and snorting through the night. Lying in bed we could hear the soft padding of jackals as they did their nightly scavenging. The odor of manure, wood smoke, spice, and flowers enveloped us in a pungent blanket. We slept soundly until the early morning sun awoke us.

Breakfast was mangoes and a flat wheat cake spread with fresh buffalo butter, then Bart and Dr. Babbar left for their hunt, accompanied by most of the men from the village. Sheila and her friends showed the boys and me over the school, and took us for a tour of the small village. It was a neat and tidy place, and obviously the villagers shared a mutual pride in their accomplishments and prosperity. The small huts were clean, the animals well cared for. Even a Dutch housewife could have found little to improve. I particularly enjoyed the chance to see the insides of village houses. Some are much more impressive than their outsides would indicate.

Steve and Tony were invited to take a ride on one of the village camels. They each tried it with such obvious enjoyment that I asked to be given a ride also. Good heavens! Gone forever is any thought of taking a camel caravan across India. Never have I been so frightened. Camels have very wide backs, and one is practically spread-eagled across them with nothing to hold onto. They rise from a kneeling position in a series of lurches which heave their passengers from one precarious position to another. Besides, they are quite unreliable animals, one minute walking along sedately, the next engaging in a race with a donkey. I didn't think I would ever be able to cling on, and was horrified to think I had let the boys ride with no hesitation. At least I provided a good deal of entertainment for the villagers. They all turned out in force to watch, and I am sure that the expression on my face made it worth their while.

The hunt was unsuccessful, but no one minded since that will give us a good excuse to make another visit.

nineteen

Khrushchev and Bulganin have been making a tour of India, and Bhakra was one of their stop-offs. We have corresponded over the months with both John Hlavacek and Alex Campbell, whose company we so much enjoyed at the time of their accident here. They wired me that they would be arriving to cover the Russians' tour, and I was determined to meet them at the train. I knew there would be dozens of foreign reporters coming in, but I could not learn just when they would arrive. I supposed they would all be with the official party, which was expected early in the morning.

Knowing the inadequate facilities on Indian trains, I packed some fruit, toast and coffee in the car, and drove as near as possible to the railroad station. The whole area was enveloped with policemen, and packed with the largest crowd I have ever seen here for foreign dignitaries. This was not precisely owing to the popularity of our visitors, but more a result of trainloads of people brought in, without charge, from surrounding towns as much as a hundred miles away. Indians love excitement of every kind. For three days, loud-speakers had patrolled Nangal, encouraging people to come out and see the fun—a message they had evidently heeded. Sneaking into the train station through the crowd made me feel like some kind of superspy.

None of the Americans here, naturally enough, were invited to be present to witness the arrival of the two Russians, and I would never have been allowed near the place if I had not become friendly with so many policemen during my months at the hospital. One by one they smiled at me and permitted me to go through the cordon surrounding the area, until I reached a good vantage point near the station steps.

The whole town had been adorned with flags and banners, while the station looked festive with new paint and bunting. The steps were lined with little girls holding white doves, to be released at the psychological moment. The doves, however, did not seem aware of their obligations, but kept escaping and fluttering off. The Russians' train finally arrived, and the two men were greeted by tremendous cheers. They wore the informal clothes and happy smiles which were to be their trademark on the trip, earning them such titles, among the Americans, as "Abbott and Costello" and "The Rover Boys." A second train had been provided for all the foreign correspondents, and was not due to arrive until later. The official train was supposed to carry only the Russian party and Indian dignitaries, but it also provided transportation for John Hlavacek and a photographer friend, who rode most of the way in the sumptuous dining car, nibbling caviar and muttering "da" to each other. The Indians supposed them to be Russians, and goodness knows what the Russians thought they were. Since John wore a bright red hunting cap, and has a face which proclaims his nationality like hot dogs and apple pie, it is hard to see how they got away with it.

I managed to attract John's attention, and he made his way to me through the crowd to slip me his story. He stayed with the official party, while I drove back to Nangal to phone in his report to New Delhi. I raced back to the station just in time to meet Alex when the reporters' train arrived. A lumbering bus, turtle-slow, had been provided for the group, but it was obvious that it would never be able to catch up with the

Russian party, now nearly an hour ahead of us, touring Bhakra. So, I picked up Alex, and several other British and American correspondents, who decided to take a chance on slipping through in my car rather than the official bus, and we started off for the dam. It was a crazy ride, and I never thought we would be able to bluff it out. Several times secret service men, in black suits and snap brim hats, halted us, but by a combined waving of press cards and a massive amount of confusion, my companions were able to convince most of them that one of our number was a Russian who had been separated from his countrymen and was now being rushed back to join them. The reporter picked for the role had been a prisoner of war in Korea, and actually spoke a little Russian, which added a touch of authenticity, although I imagine pig Latin would have served our purpose as well.

We finally caught up with the long procession of official cars, but this of course hardly satisfied my passengers. They kept urging me to get closer to the lead car carrying Khrushchev and Bulganin. I squeezed in and out of the line, displacing Governors and Maharajahs. The other drivers must have cursed me as I cut in and forced them to give us room. We finally ended up only four cars from the front. Our old Chevvy looked like somebody's country cousin in that parade of black limousines. The procession stopped every few minutes, while the Russians got out to see this or that point of interest. Each time we stopped my passengers would fly out of the car like a bunch of frantic bees, and race to the spot for pictures and quotes. It was most entertaining when in all the excitement we ran across Bart. I saw him at once, standing on one of the conveyor belt towers looking down at the show, but he refused to see me. His eyes focused on me and moved away at least a dozen times before it dawned on him that the female in the crowd was his wife. Then, of course, he got an extremely husbandly expression on his face, and I could almost hear him say, "I might have known it!"

After the tour of Bhakra, we all returned to the house, where the reporters typed out their stories, and the ones with deadlines phoned hurriedly to Delhi. Ram rose to the occasion magnificently, and hardly flicked an eyelash when I told him there would be seven extra people for lunch and dinner. The rest of the day was hectic and confused as I chauffeured the men to official luncheons, dinners and speeches. When things would seem to be calm they hurried home for coffee and to write out more stories, then went back to listen further. I marveled at the pace they all kept up, and their ability to know instinctively just which incidents would make a good story. While none of them fulfilled the layman's picture of a foreign correspondent, their insight and shrewdness concerning every facet of Indian political life was most impressive and made me ashamed of my own ignorance on the subject.

One small thing which intrigued me, and which I could not mention to the correspondents, being pledged to secrecy, was the fact that the Russians had given orders that an ambulance and doctor must accompany the official party at all times during its stay in Nangal. Perhaps this was a routine measure. Perhaps they were anticipating an assassination attempt. Or, perhaps one of the important members of the party was not in good health.

All the Americans here had been invited to the official reception for the two Russians that night, and hoping it might give them something to think about, we turned out in force. I was really proud of us at that reception. Everyone dressed tastefully and behaved charmingly, and we all infiltrated through the crowd so skillfully, one would have sworn that there were hundreds of Americans present. The Indians, as though to apologize for the show being given the Russians, were extremely cordial and friendly to us. The reception involved a number of colorful folk dances and music. Mr. Khrushchev and Mr. Bulganin seemed to enjoy it all too, and joined in every activity with great good nature, even indulging in a little horseplay on the stage when the flowers were presented. Unfortunately for us, they are most adept at this sort of thing, and I fear will make a good impression here.

At the reception's end, both Russians and correspondents entrained for the next stop on the tour, and our life settled back to normal.

Russian propagandists certainly have the advantage over us. They can claim that their country is also "Asiatic," and contend that they share the same problems as the rest of the East. While we are busy loaning money, sending wheat, and helping in a million ways to aid India, they are doling out their assistance by small handfuls. Yet they do not suffer when their aid is compared with ours because of the convincing way in which they explain their pittance. The Russians maintain, "Our country is also poor. Our people were held in bondage for centuries. Now, although we are building and growing into a great power, we are still trying to raise the standard of living of our people. We do not have very much yet, but what we have, we will share with you, our dear friends. Like you, we are struggling to surmount problems, so we understand your needs. We only wish we had more that we could give you. Still we know that shortly your country will have made tremendous advances, and you will no longer need assistance from anyone. Then we will be able to lean on your strength." This is very clever psychology. It insists that the giver is also beset by problems, and none too wealthy. It reminds the recipient that giver and receiver are allied in mutual friendship and a common struggle. It flatters the receiver that he is making such rapid progress that shortly it will be his turn to give aid.

In contrast, much of our giving seems done with the implication, "Here, take this, you poor underprivileged country. We have so much that we will hardly miss it. Of course we hardly approve of your government, nor do we have much respect for anything you are doing. If you would only let us, we could solve all your problems for you in very short order. However, we feel very sorry for you, and quite realize that you have never had our advantages. So, although we do not expect that you will ever be able to catch up with the truly civilized countries, we are generous people, and will dole out some of our wealth to come to your rescue. We trust that you will be properly grateful for our charity." Perhaps this is not the implication we intend. Perhaps such an implication does not even exist, but most Indians believe it does, and resent it wholeheartedly. While I am wholly in favor of foreign aid, I am completely opposed to foreign charity. It is a grave error to give to any country which we do not sincerely respect, as it is an error to anticipate that our aid will buy us a single friend. Friendship cannot exist when one partner is made to feel inferior, and the very fact that a country needs our aid supposes its inferiority. We have made a serious mistake in so blatantly advertising all the best aspects of our American way of life in its richness and plenty. Our purpose would be better served if we allowed other countries an insight into the problems we face, if we permitted them to know that we are not endlessly rich, if we asked their advice in the struggles we face.

Our blithe assurance that we have all the answers is not endearing. We would gain a hundred friends if we asked help, for every one we gain by giving help. This help need not be material, and certainly not military, but an exchange of advice and ideas which would enable the poorer country to feel that it had a worthwhile contribution to make as part of a friendship. We should come to an understanding and humble appreciation of the fact that every people has something to offer us, that only when we approach them with respect and sincerity will they appreciate the worth of what we have to offer. In that way, we could say to a country like India, "Here, let us help you get rid of your malaria, but in return we wonder if you would be willing to give us some advice on the problem of increased drug addiction we are facing?" or, "Look, our juvenile crime rate is increasing at an alarming rate. How do you handle this problem?"

or, "We both have a great deal of work to do in slum clearance. If you will tell us how you are planning to approach the matter, we will give you our ideas."

The Communists are clever. In this part of the world, they are using words better than we. Unless we revise our thinking quickly, we may doom yet another section of mankind to live without the freedom which is humanity's greatest treasure.

twenty

The days have gone by here, and I have hardly marked the seasons. We had an Indian circus in town for a week, which presented such an opportunity for entertainment that we all saw it several times. A circus is a circus in any country, and to me this one-ring show had the sort of excitement I remember from my childhood, a quality many of our more lavish circuses have lost. There were really funny clowns who hit each other with paddles. These monkeyshines so carried Tony away at one performance that he left his seat, ran into the ring, and got in a lick or two himself, before we dragged him back. They had a motorcyclist who rode off into space from a high ramp, and they had acrobats, trapeze artists, and all the required animals. We treated a number of the performers for mild ailments at the hospital, and I was able to talk the manager into giving me half-price seats for our ambulatory patients. Some of the patients who attended were scarcely able to stand, much less walk; in fact every case who was not actually critically ill talked me into including him. Along with wheel chairs and stretchers, we loaded group after group into the ambulance and took them to the circus tents. Many of the patients told me, "Mem-sahib, I stay here, you take my little boy instead." Or they had a wife, mother, or daughter they preferred to have go in their place.

Naturally these tactics worked perfectly, and the original count grew to include innumerable sons, daughters, grandmothers, cousins and uncles. Since most of the hospital staff, along with their families, also accompanied us, it was quite a crowd. The preliminary ticket buying was really an ordeal. The patients milled around the circus tents tripping over each other's crutches, and causing me to worry that they would all be mangled dreadfully in the crush. Every time I tried to count noses and buy the tickets, someone would shout, "You didn't count those people, Mem-sahib. They are with us." Strange children surrounded me on every side, pulling at my skirt, and begging me to buy them a ticket too. Eventually almost everyone in sight ended up going in with us. But, oh, what a wonderful time we all had! The bedridden stay-behinds were brought balloons and candy, and are still being treated to enthusiastic imitations of how the lions roared and how the clowns behaved.

For a week or so I have become temporary mother for a baby boy found on one of the canal banks. We never knew how he got there, but someone must have hoped he would be discovered, since he was warmly wrapped. It was a wonder that the jackals did not carry him off before we found him. The police brought him to the hospital, and I carried him home, since the nurses have no way of fixing formulas, or time to attend carefully a motherless baby. The whole family enjoyed the new addition, and the boys named him Joe. I would have liked to keep him, but there are many difficulties involved in adopting a foreign child, and Bart kept reminding me that one baby at a time was all he felt able to stand.

We had numerous applicants who wanted to adopt little Joe, and it was hard to know which one to choose. Dr. Babbar felt that the hospital cook and his wife, who is sterile, were best able to care for him, so with reluctance I turned the child over to them. I still see him every day at the hospital, and gave his new mother a supply of baby things and plenty of vitamin drops.

We have half-adopted another boy, a thirteen-year-old. He knows he cannot go home with us, but he has become nearly ours for the time we are here. He was a patient at the hospital for some time, suffering from tuberculosis of the knee joint. He is an orphan and had no one to bring him food or care for him. His disease is a chronic one which sometimes takes years to cure entirely. When he was advised to leave the hospital and come back again in three months, he had nowhere to go. I got Dr. Babbar to X-ray his chest and make a sputum test, both of which were negative, so he moved in with us. He has been going to school, and his knee is improving rapidly.

I found out a short time ago that Persinni, Jugetram's wife, is also expecting a baby. She has certainly managed to conceal the fact. I have been making shirts and kimonos for both babies, and whenever I take her some, she giggles and covers her face. Jugetram blushes whenever he looks at me. They want another boy, and assure me that I will have a son also.

The Indian villagers' method of child rearing is remarkable. They seem to have been putting into practice for years all the things our child psychologists have just discovered. In this district, Indian village parents are completely permissive. Babies, from the time they are born, are allowed to do and have whatever they want. They are seldom refused or thwarted in any way, and the whole family, from the parents to the youngest child, spends most of the time petting, feeding, coddling and entertaining the baby. No attempt is made to wean or toilet-train a baby until he is old enough to do it himself. Many children still nurse at two and three. Eventually another infant arrives to supplant the youngest, yet jealousy does not seem to be a problem. The recently pampered baby now joins with the family in pleasing its newest member, with every evidence of deep affection. Presumably, each child is made to feel so secure within the family group that a new baby poses no threat.

Indian children even play differently from ours. I seldom hear them quarreling or fighting. They are very unaggressive, and never seem to find sharing with each other a problem. Nathan is so much Indian in this respect that he automatically gives part of every cookie, banana, or mango which he is given to Bimela and Caca. He will not even accept a toy or a piece of clothing from us unless we provide the equivalent for his two little playmates.

The harshest words I have ever heard a villager use to his child were, "No, no, my sweet darling," spoken in a loving croon. Sometimes the love of Indian parents for their children causes us trouble at the hospital when a father or mother will refuse to have a sick child operated upon, or even given an injection, through fear of causing it pain. However, a sympathetic explanation of what we want to do usually calms their fears. Either despite, or because of this apparent spoiling, Indian children seem happy, well adjusted, affectionate and unselfish. On the other hand, they are more placid, less independent, less competitive and less stoic than ours. Even as they grow older the contrast with our children is apparent. I recently passed out packages of colored pencils and pads of paper to several teen-age boys who are bedridden at the hospital. I thought that drawing pictures might help pass the time for them. When they showed me their drawings several days later each one had covered pages with exquisite flower studies. I know too well the scenes our boys pick to draw: jet airplanes, football games, battles at sea— but flowers? never! Yet these boys must certainly have been exposed to scenes of violence during partition.

Well we had another boy, just as I knew we would. I wondered during the last months if I would be disappointed if no daughter appeared, but I was not—not in the least. We have named him John Benjamin, but are calling him Jay. He has such long eyelashes that they get all tangled up in his tiny brows.

My friend Tej Lamba, and Sheila Babbar kept me company through most of it, and Bart stayed in the delivery room. Dr. Babbar is Jay's godfather, and following the Hindu custom he gave him a gold ring dipped in honey to suck for his first meal. Persinni had her baby, also a boy, soon after I had mine. She is unable to nurse, so I have been boiling bottles and making formulas for her little one. The Indians are quite scandalized at our barbaric American custom of permitting a new mother to resume normal life so rapidly after her confinement. Even very poor Indian women have numerous female relatives who come and take over all the new mother's duties and permit her to rest after having a baby. The period of rest is traditionally forty days, although this is not followed as rigidly as formerly. The new mother is given special rich food and is the center of attention for the whole family clan, especially if she has given birth to a son. My Indian friends even disapproved of my reading, as being too mentally strenuous for a maternity case. I don't know how the Indian custom compares to ours physically in its result on the health of mothers. But this I do know—Indian women never suffer from postnatal depression!

The days seem to fly by. I have an ayah to help with the baby, and she is a dear, but since I am nursing him, I still have to be around a great deal. He is a greedy little glutton. The boys are quite delighted with their new brother, and informed me that, "We never did want an old girl in this family, anyway!" Nathan is happy that both Bimela and he each have a new baby at the same time. He probably thinks things are arranged that way for his satisfaction. I never get time to write now. It is much more fun to play with the baby.

Tony has been terribly ill. I can hardly write about it even now. He picked up tetanus through a small wound in his heel, and I think he would have died without Dr. Babbar. Bart and I have never been so utterly terrified. I have nursed cases of tet-

anus, here in the hospital, and know well what it can do. For
two days Dr. Babbar hardly left Tony's side, while Sheila and
Tej Lamba stayed with me. It was particularly hard for the
Babbars, since it reminded them of the little son they lost a few
years ago in a similar experience.

Everyone was wonderful. Both Indian and our American
friends have helped in every possible way. Tony's teacher,
Rachael Beavers, sat by his side for hours when I was unable to
keep myself under control. Poor little Tony. He is quite recovered and happy now, but Bart and I are still shaken and
afraid. I have been so casual about life here, but now I feel
nervous about every little thing and worry about each separate
child, as though none of them were safe. My first reaction was
a desire to leave at once, and though I have got over the worst
of that, going home still appeals to me. I know the fact that he
became so ill in India does not mean anything. He could have
picked up the same infection in the States or been hit by a car.
Still I suppose it is natural to want to go home and lick your
wounds when disaster strikes, and that is how I feel.

twenty-one

We have decided to leave here in time to be home for Christmas. We were going to leave next spring in any case, and the coming of the Christmas season has made us all homesick, as it always does. Why not leave now? Why not have Christmas at home? The more we think about it, the nicer it sounds. Since Jay was born, and since Tony was so ill, we have felt more and more that the time was coming to leave. Our contract with the Punjab government was completed six months ago, so there is nothing to hold us here except our love for the place and the people. This affection is going to make leaving here difficult, whenever we go.

The ordeal of packing trunks, typing lists, making travel arrangements, and generally getting ready has started, but instead of keeping me at home, the knowledge that we are leaving soon drives me to spend every possible minute at the hospital. The days go by and I can count them off, thirty days, twenty-five days, twenty days. I know as I walk through the wards that I will leave India before many of the patients leave the hospital, and I will never know how successfully they recovered. I look around at my special pets, the children, and wonder if this leg will knit, if this operation will succeed, if this child will ever be able to walk.

We have had two very interesting cases in the past couple of weeks. Our two patients were both from the same part of the world, but there their similarity ends. One we lost, but the other we were able to help. The first man was brought in unconscious from Bhakra and dumped on us without ceremony. He appeared to be either Tibetan or Nepalese, but he was obviously a stranger to these parts, and no one seemed to know him. He was without a single friend. We put him to bed preparatory to diagnosing him, and he regained consciousness long enough for us to realize that whatever language he spoke, it was not one that a single person in the hospital could understand. Even his name remained a mystery. He had been hired at Bhakra as a coolie only a few days before, and collapsed on the job with no forewarning. He fell back into a coma, and the doctors discovered that he was an advanced case of tuberculosis of the lungs who gave every appearance of lapsing into tubercular meningitis. This really put us in a difficult position. We sometimes accept cases of tuberculosis of the bone, or of the glands, which are not infectious. But we have no way of isolating a patient with a contagious lung involvement, and the crowded conditions here make it very risky to treat such a case.

Usually we would have returned such a patient to his family with as much advice and medicine as we had to give, or permitted his relatives to keep him in our isolation hut and care for him there. But this man had no family or friends to turn to, and we could hardly push him out of the hospital to die on the streets. Dr. Babbar wanted to send him to the isolation hut in charge of one of the sweepers, but admitted that none of them would give him the kind of expert nursing he had to have in his comatose state. I prevailed upon him to permit the man to stay in the hospital, isolated, as well as could be, on one of the outside verandas. There his condition became worse and worse, almost by the hour. He had no control over his urine or feces and his bed soon became a horrible mess. He coughed and spat blood, and of course was unable to feed himself or take water.

The staff avoided him and I could not blame them—he was not only an unpleasant nursing problem, but obviously highly infectious. I bought some streptomycin injections for him, despite advice to save the money for a patient with a better chance to live. Indeed, it was hopeless, but I felt we should do everything we could for this stranger, and guilty at my own inability to tend him. I am still nursing Jay, and every time I so much as stood near the patient's bed, I felt a terrible fear that I would carry back some stray bacteria to the baby. Dr. Babbar did not help when he caught me gingerly sponging the man's face, and threatened to bar me from the hospital if I so much as touched him again.

He had to be kept clean, and constantly given fluids to prevent the dehydration that would have been the final straw in his condition, but no one would do these things. Indeed, it would have been most unwise to have the nurses and ward servants tend to him and then go on to assist other patients. Dr. Babbar was worried at the patient's condition and at the prevalence of flies drawn to his bed, then buzzing off to carry the contagion elsewhere. To send him to the isolation hut at this point was to condemn him to certain death from neglect.

Finally, I took the problem to Ram, and told him to find someone—anyone—who would sit by his side, feed him, sponge him, and give him fluids. As an inducement, I offered to pay five rupees a day to anyone willing to perform these functions. I thought for a moment Ram would insist on going himself, since this is more salary than he makes as a cook, but he was contented with grumbling, "Too much money, Mem-sahib-ji." After a couple of false starts with applicants who were interested in the five rupees but not in the work they would have to do to earn it, we finally found a young man willing to assume the risk. I got a facial mask for him, and Dr. Babbar showed him how to spoon fluids into the patient's grimacing mouth. We both issued stern warnings to keep as clear as possible from the coughing, and to wash his hands constantly. I felt better about the case, but then started to worry about the man I had hired, and the risk I had bribed him to run.

Our patient lingered for days, rallying slightly, then deteriorating again. We pushed tremendous injections of streptomycin and penicillin into his emaciated arms, knowing he was too far gone, but hoping desperately that he could hang on long enough for the drugs to help. Ram carried over broth and lemonade, and I watched from a distance, listening to the patient's labored breathing. Soon the whole hospital was united in concern for his life. Every night I went over several times to see if he was still keeping up the struggle to live, and each time I found a group of silent watchers gathered nearby in silent vigil. The young man I had hired cared for him gently and compassionately, which made me ashamed of my own nervousness. Finally one morning, our unknown patient died. When I entered the hospital the Assistant Surgeon met me with a sad face and the nurses all looked away. I knew what had happened, and felt the same feeling of failure and loss that I saw on their faces. No one would take any money from me to buy firewood. Instead, the members of the staff got together the necessary rupees, and burned his body in a Hindu ceremony by the edge of the river. We wondered if he had been a Hindu. It seemed more likely that he was a Buddhist, but no one knew what the Buddhist rites might be. The saddest part of all was the fact that we still did not know his name. The ashes of our unknown patient were consigned to the water, and I wondered if somewhere far away his family was waiting for him. It seems too cruel that they will never know what happened to him, but will go on waiting, month after month, for his expected return.

Our second patient, far from being unknown, was an illustrious personage indeed, the Lord High Chamberlain of Tibet. He was admitted to our hospital not of his own accord, but because he was visiting Nangal just when his appendix decided

to give trouble. The Dalai Lama of Tibet made his first trip
out of his country, and accompanied by a large entourage, paid
a royal visit to India. A friend of Dr. Babbar, who is in charge
of the secret service arrangements for visits of this kind, told us
that the visit of the Dalai Lama presented a graver problem in
diplomatic arrangements than Bulganin and Khrushchev, or
any other guest so entertained by the state. Because of the
Lama's religious eminence in the Buddhist hierarchy, the slight-
est mishap in his reception could have dramatic and serious con-
sequences. Then too, he numbered in his party a group of silent
Chinese, presumed to be his communist watchdogs, who would
be eager to snatch at any pretext to isolate him again, or to try
to persuade him that the tiniest incident was a deliberate Indian
affront, in order to bind him more closely to their own country
and alienate him even further from Tibet's only other important neighbor.

So the arrangements for the Dalai Lama's visit to Bhakra were
carefully planned and nearly secret. There could be none of
the entertainments usually presented, since it was necessary to
isolate him from all contact with women, and since his religious
devotion made such frivolous doings unacceptable. He arrived,
with his large party, made a tour of Bhakra, ate a quiet luncheon, rested, and was due to leave on a special train, when his
older brother, the Lord High Chamberlain, complained of an
intense pain in his abdomen. I knew nothing of the succeeding
hours until late that night. Dr. Babbar avoided me, made
numerous hurried telephone calls in rapid Punjabi, and when
he looked at me at all, did so as though I were a stranger who
had unaccountably stumbled into his presence. I was exceed-
ingly puzzled, and went home to meditate on my sins and figure
out just which particular one had caused his hostility. Later on
I found out that he had been pledged to secrecy, and I realized
how hard such a pledge was for him to keep, under my alert
eyes.

By evening, I was itching with curiosity, as strange cars

pulled mysteriously into the hospital compound and Indian notables huddled together in the corridors. Though neither Indians nor Tibetans could be expected to know it, this was my hospital they were involving in their peculiar intrigues. After dinner I walked up to the hospital, now suddenly quiet, and then on to Dr. Babbar's house where the strange cars were now much in evidence. Poor Dr. Babbar greeted me at his door with as much eagerness as he might a hooded cobra, but the damage was done. I spied Colonel Bhatia, the Chief Medical Officer from Chandigarh, whose excellent company we had several times enjoyed, sitting in the living room. "What in the world are you doing here?" I asked him. "What is going on?" "Doesn't Carol know about it all?" Colonel Bhatia in turn asked Dr. Babbar. Then seeing that quite obviously I didn't he proceeded to explain at once.

When the Dalai Lama had sent for Dr. Babbar to examine his brother, the doctor had immediately diagnosed an acute attack of appendicitis. The Lord High Chamberlain was in violent pain, his white blood count was very high, and there could be no doubt as to the diagnosis. Dr. Babbar gave him a massive dose of penicillin, and what palliative treatment he could, then notified both Indian and Tibetan officials that the patient had a very ugly appendix which seemed likely to rupture unless an operation were performed at once. It is difficult to describe the consternation that this problem caused. To us, it seems a comparatively simple matter to remove the offending appendix, but there was a great deal more than that involved. Indian government officials were panic-stricken at the responsibility suddenly forced upon them. If the Lama's brother were operated upon, and the operation was unsuccessful, all sorts of unpleasant diplomatic crises might result. If, on the other hand, no operation were performed and the man should die on Indian soil, it might be even worse. There seemed a risk either way. The Tibetans, to complicate matters, have had little contact with modern medicine, and practically no knowledge of surgery. They viewed the possibility of an operation with the utmost distrust, and had so far refused to contemplate such a procedure. Several Buddhist monks had been consulted within their group, and by an elaborate method of prognostication in which small black and white balls were juggled, the monks foretold that the omens were quite adverse to performing surgery.

The situation had reached a stalemate when I arrived at Dr. Babbar's house, and there it seemed destined to remain. The Chief Surgeon from Amritsar had been summoned but had not yet arrived. Each new doctor who examined the patient echoed Dr. Babbar and said, "Operate," at which the monks tossed their small balls around even more violently and said, "Don't operate!" A special car arranged for the patient's comfort had been connected to the official train. The Lama agreed that his party would delay their departure until ten P.M. in the hope that his brother's attack would subside by then. That hour had almost arrived, and far from subsiding, the pain was as intense as ever. The Indian doctors were extremely worried about the risk of permitting such a patient to be jostled about in a train for eleven hours, and all too aware that once he left Nangal, there would be no other hospital on his route before New Delhi. Even if one or both of the doctors accompanied him, should the appendix rupture during the trip, there would be little they could do. All over the Punjab, every Indian official not already in Nangal was rushing in our direction, while the telephone jangled constantly with long-distance calls from New Delhi and all points south.

Actually His Holiness the Lama and his entourage had already boarded the train, where his brother had been made as comfortable as possible, when the doctors decided to make one last effort. They went to the station, and appealed to the Lama to permit the Lord Chamberlain to remain behind for a day or two of rest, promising that no operation would be performed unless his condition worsened. I believe that the Lama was eager to find a solution that would aid his brother without antagonizing other members of his party, for he readily agreed to the proposal. In fact, he skillfully opened the door for us when he said, "You have our permission to operate at any time, should you think it has become necessary." I think he knew that we had every intention of operating at once, unless there was a miraculous recovery, and chose this way to let us know that he approved, while at the same time leaving the responsibility for the decision up to the doctors involved. The sick man and a small group of Tibetans left the train and were taken by ambulance to the hospital.

None of us got much sleep that night. The official party left on the train, and I received the impression from both the Indian doctors and the officials I met, for of course I had no contact with the Lama, that he was determined to prevent the accident of his brother's illness being used in any way to thwart his visit to India, with the friendship such a visit implied. Our work at the hospital to accommodate such a royal group was most difficult. We have no rooms of the high standard that would usually be expected, and in the middle of the night we were still scurrying about trying to locate rugs, chairs and extra beds to make the party more comfortable. The most amusing of their requests came very late that night when the translator informed us that some beer would be appreciated. This request caught the Indians off guard, and it was quite a scramble to awaken the shopkeeper of the only liquor store in the bazaar, and buy from him this unexpected beverage. The usual governmental complications developed when the various department heads involved began to wonder just who should be paying for these extras. Each official felt strongly that every effort should be made to give our unexpected guests every possible luxury, but was just as certain that his particular branch of the government could hardly be involved in paying for it. Finally, everyone agreed that each request would be met, and everything necessary purchased, while the ultimate accounting would wait until later. I imagine it will be years before the matter of who should pay for the beer will be straightened out.

Late in the night, Dr. Santosh Singh, the Senior Surgeon from Amritsar, arrived with three nurses. Again the patient was examined, and again the doctors agreed that an operation was urgently needed, since the severity of the attack showed no sign of abating. The hours were passing by, and each hour increased the risk involved in surgery. They decided to operate in the morning, not so many hours away, unless there was radical improvement. After the long day we all caught a little much needed sleep, while Colonel Bhatia's excellent Matron, a fine nurse, stayed with the patient.

In the morning the Dalai Lama was again reached by phone, and received the report that his brother's condition remained alarming. He repeated his permission to operate, and we proceeded immediately. Our poor patient was terribly frightened at the prospect of surgery, an emotion we certainly understood later when he showed us scars on his body where he had been burned with hot irons for similar pains in the past, evidently the Tibetan form of surgery. We learned that our patient's modesty would make it impossible for us to bathe and prepare him for the operation in the usual way, so this procedure had to wait until he was under anesthetic on the operating table. Dr. Santosh Singh performed the operation, with Colonel Bhatia and Dr. Babbar assisting. The Chief Surgeon used his own nurses brought with him for the purpose. I stayed in the operating theater, mostly as a repository of various eyeglasses and wrist watches, and as a messenger to reassure the waiting Tibetans that "The Lord High Chamberlain has reacted well to the anesthetic and is now sleeping quietly," or, "The operation has begun and is going smoothly." The appendix, when they finally reached it, fully justified the doctors' fears. It was hugely swollen and already tinged green with gangrene. But it was soon removed. The whole operation was in every way routine with no complications, for which everyone was most grateful.

The Tibetan translator, to whom by necessity I directed my reassurances, was a fascinating figure. Tall and slender, he wore his hair in long, thin braids wound round and round his head. He was dressed in a full-length padded garment, and wore one turquoise earring which dangled below his shoulder. He was permitted to enter the theater several times during the operation to take pictures of the proceedings with his excellent camera. When the operation had progressed to the routine stitching of the incision, I stayed out on the veranda and chatted with him. His English was precise and idiomatic, with less British inflection than most Indians retain. Although I had been wearing saris during the whole episode, he had discovered my nationality, and asked me questions about the United States. I had no way of knowing what his politics might be, so I tried to make my answers friendly and casual. The one Chinese who had stayed behind with the group soon joined us, and by his knowing smile at some of my remarks, I felt certain that he, too, understood English. Shortly, he joined our conversation when a response of mine concerning the number of automobiles in our country seemed to annoy him. With the same smile, he asked in English, "Is it not true that the poor workers in your country do not own cars?" I smiled back, and replied, "Very few workers in our country do not own cars, and many workers have two cars." After this exchange, I felt it would be wise to remain uninvolved further, and removed myself. I was all too aware of my peculiar position. As a personal friend of all three doctors involved, and of several of the Indian dignitaries concerned, I had been permitted to occupy a grandstand seat for this whole affair, and included in all the behind the scenes discussions and worries that it had entailed. The Indians had problems enough in diplomacy during this unexpected incident without adding any needless embarrassment because of my nationality. I spoke to the interpreter a number of times in the following days. He remained enigmatic though friendly. I avoided the Chinese gentleman, and exchanged only polite nods with him thereafter.

Our patient made a quick recovery. The other doctors returned to their own district hospitals leaving us in charge of his postoperative care. The young Lord High Chamberlain (he was in his early twenties) seemed wholeheartedly delighted with his operation, and the break in routine that his stay in our hospital involved. He seized every opportunity to chat with the doctors, and even conquered his modesty sufficiently to lift the ban on nurses entering his room. When he became well enough to walk about, he asked permission to watch us operate, and was enthralled when he saw us remove another appendix, in the same operation he had undergone. He suggested that Dr. Babbar examine his throat, which he said pained him a great deal, and was positively gratified to learn that he had very badly infected tonsils. Soon he was making happy plans to return to us, with his brother's permission, and have these removed also.

We were fortunate that our young Tibetan friend had a strong stomach, while his Chinese companion did not. As a result, during the time he was with us in the operating theater, he was alone, which led to the most interesting conversation I enjoyed with him. After a lengthy morning in surgery, on the day before he was to leave us, Dr. Babbar suggested that he join the two of us for coffee. He seemed to hesitate for a moment, but agreed, and with the interpreter, who never left his side, we went out by a side door and into the doctor's private dressing room. I made coffee on our hot plate, and we sat around the table together drinking it. Dr. Babbar let me enjoy most of the conversation, since I had not had his opportunity to talk much with the young man. I began, as innocuously as possible, by telling him how interested I was in his language, which seemed nothing like the oriental sing-song I had expected, but had instead many of the sounds and inflexions heard in English. I went on to tell him how very intrigued Americans were by his country and its customs; how we read books about it and studied it in school. He replied that his people were equally curious about my country, and very much regretted that there was not more contact between us. He paused for a moment, then spoke to the translator, with a certain urgency. "He would like to know if you are acquainted with an American, Mr. Lowell Thomas," said the translator. I answered that I did not know Mr. Thomas, personally, but certainly knew who he was, as he was a very well known person in America. The Lord High Chamberlain listened carefully to the translation of this, then spoke again, "I would like Mr. Thomas to know that he is very much remembered in Tibet. I, myself, talked to him while he visited us, and in our country we speak of him and his son very often." He went on to ask me what both Mr. Thomas and his son were now doing, and I racked my brains trying to remember things I had read of their activities. He seemed to be unaware of the book the Thomases had written about their visit to Tibet, and was very pleased to hear my account of how widely it was read, and how very happy Americans were to receive news of his country. I promised that I would see that Mr. Thomas heard of his message, feeling certain that our newspaper friend, John Hlavacek, would know how to go about this—which he later did.

The two Tibetans seemed to feel that perhaps they had played truant long enough. I still was unable to figure out the translator's position regarding the various people he served, and could not be certain how much constraint his presence added to the talk. As they made a move to go, the Lord High Chamberlain said again, "We very much hope that someday many more Americans like Mr. Thomas will visit our country. It is our deep wish that we can be friends." I told him that this was a wish all Americans sincerely shared. Then he took a pen and a small bit of paper torn from a pad on the table, and wrote a few Tibetan letters. As he handed it to me, the translator explained that the letters stood for our American phrase, "Good luck." The young man nodded at me earnestly, and I, in turn, wrote the same phrase in English on another scrap, and handed it to him, wishing ardently that my handwriting were more impressive. I said, "Good luck to you and to Tibet," which he seemed to understand without translation. He folded the paper, and put it carefully in his pocket, his eyes watching my face intently. I felt moved by all the implications suggested by the two of us wishing "good luck" to each other and his country, and wondered if this small exchange was as important to him as it appeared to be. We looked at each other for a few seconds, and I hope my face mirrored the sincerity and grave understanding I saw on his. Then he turned and left and I did not have a chance to speak with him again.

Those were the two patients, probably the last two who will be important to me before we leave. One had no name while the other had an impressive title, one we lost and one we saved, but for each we had done what we could.

twenty-two

During the two and a half years we have been here, we have made the trip to the little train station many times to say goodbye to American friends who were leaving Nangal. Now, it is our turn. We have been so busy making all our travel preparations, packing trunks and suitcases, being entertained, that only for brief periods has the fact that we were actually leaving really held any meaning. But, last night at the railroad station when we actually said goodbye, it suddenly occurred to all of us that this was the kind of farewell seldom said. We could leave American friends with at least a hope of seeing them again. But when we said goodbye to all the Indians we had grown so fond of, we could not give them the construction workers' farewell, "Hope we make another job together," or "See you on the next dam." Our goodbyes to our Indian friends had to be very final. Saying goodbye to the servants was the hardest of all. Persinni buried her head on my shoulder and sobbed. Bimela, with her little face swollen from crying, wound her arms around my neck and would not let go. Ram stood by like a stricken statue, repeating over and over, "Mem-sahib, take me with you. Please let me go too."

To each of them I promised again and again, "Someday we will come back and see you," knowing even as I said the words

175

that I might never be able to keep the promise. I know Ram will be all right. We have found him a job with another American family, and he has his house and a buffalo in his village. Ram has saved a good part of his salary while working for us, and is frugal enough to make it last for a long time. But I worry about Jugetram and his family. He was a bearer for us, but no one else here needs a bearer now, and I am afraid he will once again be a sweeper, with a salary only large enough to cover the barest necessities of existence. I have left him enough money to carry them for several months, and I pleaded with him to use it wisely. But I cannot be sure that it will not be spent for new earrings for Persinni and a big gold watch for Jugetram. He has not Ram's shrewd good sense where money is concerned. The Babbars and Margaret and Raj Garg have both promised to look after the servants, but it gives me a helpless feeling to know that I will be so far away and so ignorant of their fates. As we stepped on the train and looked down on all the beloved faces, I wanted to get off at once and reassure them that we would not leave after all. I suddenly had a most terrible sensation, and thought to myself, "Why, I am leaving part of the family behind! How can I bear to desert children I love as much as my own? What am I doing?" But it was too late. The train had started to move slowly along the tracks. We stood at the open door looking back at all we were leaving behind. Atma Singh, Bart's wonderful foreman, with his strong Sikh face and kind eyes, stood with his hand raised in a half salute. Dr. Babbar and Margaret and Raj, dear friends, were grouped together, silently watching us. I wanted to call to Dr. Babbar, "Don't forget we must order more cholera vaccine. Please watch that head injury case for me. Let me know how that cancer patient does." A million unspoken words raced through my head, and a thousand things I had wanted to do at the hospital and never completed came back to haunt me. Some of the men who had worked for Bart ran along beside the train shouting their farewells. The American children called last minute jokes to our excited boys. And our servants huddled together in a miserable knot, still crying out, "Mem-sahib, don't leave us, don't leave us."

This morning Bart and I both feel empty of emotion and dry of tears. The children are chattering happily of the plane trip home. And we are thinking of spending Christmas with our families in our own country for the first time in three years. Bart has said over and over, "We had to leave them sometime. It would not be any easier a few months from now. They will all forget us quickly, and give their love to some other family soon." And this is true. We must look ahead to the future, and that is not hard to do when the future means going home, and being with friends and relatives whom we have missed over here. I know I may never see India again. I may never see the friends and all the people I love who mean India to me. But as much as one can love a country not his own, I love India. Someday I mean to come back. In the meantime, I hope that her friendship for our country will grow, and her problems diminish, but I know that the goodness of her people will never change.

"Liberty will not descend to a people. A people must raise themselves to liberty. It is a blessing that must be earned before it can be enjoyed."
                        Inscription on the Indian Parliament Building

Goodbye and Good Luck. May you not seek an easier path, but rather continue to solve your problems with a constant regard for the liberty of your people.